Sixth Edition

# Hard Choices for Loving People

CPR,

Feeding Tubes,

Palliative Care,

Comfort Measures,

and the Patient

with a Serious Illness

**By Hank Dunn**
Chaplain

Front cover design by Paul A. Gormont, Apertures, Inc., Sterling, VA
Cover photo of the Chesapeake Bay by Helmuth Humphrey

To purchase books, for more information, or for a full list of citations
and references related to the topics discussed in this book, visit
### www.hankdunn.com

Also available by Hank Dunn:

*Hard Choices for Loving People*
in Spanish, Chinese, and Japanese

*Light in the Shadows:*
*Meditations While Living with a*
*Life-Threatening Illness*

Published by:

Quality of Life Publishing Co., 6210 Shirley Street, Suite 112, Naples, FL 34109

Toll Free: (877) 513-0099 | Phone: (239) 513-9907 | Fax: (239) 513-0088

www.QOLpublishing.com

Quality of Life Publishing Co. is an independent publisher
specializing in branded educational materials for healthcare and end-of-life care,
as well as books that educate, inspire, and motivate.

**ISBN: 978-0-9972612-0-2**

## Millions of copies sold worldwide.

*Hard Choices for Loving People* has sold over 3.8 million copies.
This bestselling book is now in its 6th edition, and is used by more than
5,000 hospitals, nursing homes, faith communities, and hospice programs
internationally for over 30 years.

*Light in the Shadows* is a collection of reflections on the emotional and
spiritual concerns of those facing serious illness. Now in its 2nd edition, this
valuable companion book has been in publication for over 15 years.

# About the Author

Since 1983, Hank Dunn has been ministering to patients at the end of their lives and their families. He served as a nursing home chaplain at Fairfax Nursing Center and as a staff chaplain for the Hospice of Northern Virginia, now Capital Hospice.

In 1990, Hank wrote a booklet to help explain end-of-life decisions to patients and families and encourage reflection on the issues discussed. As an afterthought, he sent the booklet out to other institutions to see if they would be interested in purchasing it for the people they serve. Interest in the material grew and Hank's first book, *Hard Choices for Loving People,* was born.

Hank is a graduate of the University of Florida and received his Master of Divinity degree from the Southern Baptist Theological Seminary in Louisville, Kentucky. After serving five years as a youth minister at a very traditional church in Macon, Georgia, he moved to the DC area to be a part of the very nontraditional Church of the Saviour. He worked a year as a carpenter and for four years directed an inner city ministry before moving into the chaplaincy in 1983.

He is a past president of the Northern Virginia Chapter of the Alzheimer's Association. He has served on the Ethics Committee at the Reston Hospital Center and the Chaplaincy Advisory Board at the Loudoun Hospital Center.

For several years, Chaplain Dunn volunteered at Joseph's House, a home for formerly homeless men and women who are terminally ill. He was also a Volunteer Pastoral Associate at Vienna Baptist Church, where he was especially involved in the retreat ministry at the Lost River Retreat Center in West Virginia. He has also volunteered as a chaplain at the Loudoun Hospital and at the Loudoun Adult Medical Psychiatric Services.

Hank Dunn is a frequent speaker on topics related to serious illness and the end of life. He enjoys backpacking, kayaking, and hiking.

# Contents

# Introduction

On the occasion of her 102nd birthday, I visited Mable in her room at the nursing home to ask her the secret to a long life. Since she was a minister's wife, I expected some niceties like "clean living" or "just trust God." But she was too wise for that. "Mable, how do you live to be 102?" I asked. Without hesitation she responded, "Just keep breathing!"

I wish it were so easy. If we want to stay alive, we "just keep breathing." Or when there is no hope of recovery from an illness, we could "just stop breathing." Real life is not so simple for patients who find themselves moving toward the end of a long decline in their health.

Throughout most of our life, medical treatment decisions are quite simple. We get sick. Our doctor prescribes a treatment. Since we expect to benefit from the physician's orders, we follow the treatment plan and return to our previous state of health.

Yet as our health declines, medical decisions become more complex. Patients who have multiple medical problems, who depend on others for daily care (like nursing home residents), or who have a terminal condition often face difficult treatment choices.

For patients with a serious or long-term chronic illness, some medical treatments offer little benefit. These treatments may be painful or increase the burden of living. This makes healthcare decisions more difficult, because we must constantly weigh possible benefits against possible burdens of a particular treatment plan. Sometimes people conclude that the burdens far outweigh any possible benefit, and they therefore refuse a particular treatment. Others feel that even a small potential benefit is worth the significant burdens.

Today's generations are the first to be faced with making such difficult choices about potentially life-prolonging medical treatments. Modern medical developments like ventilators, feeding tubes, and cardiopulmonary resuscitation (CPR) have improved the odds for some of surviving an accident, heart attack, or stroke.

*It is very important that patients and their families discuss the use of life-prolonging medical procedures.*

But the declining health of patients with multiple medical problems—or of those with a terminal condition—make the chance of survival much poorer than that of the general public. Therefore, it is very important that all seriously ill patients and their families discuss the use of life-prolonging medical procedures.

**This book is written to provide guidance to patients and their families facing "hard choices" as they receive and participate in healthcare.** The goal is to give enough information to help make informed decisions.

### The Four Most Common Decisions

Some of the hardest choices about medical care that patients and families must face can be summarized in four questions:[1]

1. Shall resuscitation be attempted? (see pages 7–12)
2. Shall artificial nutrition and hydration (a feeding tube) be used? (see pages 13–24)
3. Should a patient be transferred from their place of residence to a hospital? (see pages 37–39)
4. Is it time to shift the treatment goal from cure to hospice or comfort measures only? (see pages 28–36)

Besides these four more common decisions, some attention will also be given in this book to palliative care, ventilators (breathing machines), dialysis, antibiotics, pacemakers and implanted defibrillators, and pain control. Consideration will be given for how these treatments affect different patients, including children or those with dementia (for example, Alzheimer's). After a thoughtful reading of these pages, you may want to discuss what is contained here with your family and physician.

Although I draw from medical research and my professional experience with these decisions, I can only make general suggestions about treatment options. I recommend discussing available medical treatments with your physician and other healthcare professionals familiar with your particular situation. My experiences may not address the specific circumstances you are facing. All the stories I share are true, although I have changed certain names to protect privacy.

## Goals of Medical Care

Before thinking about potentially life-prolonging medical procedures, it's important to establish the goal of medical care.[2] **Ask yourself, "What outcome can we reasonably expect from medical treatment, given the current condition of the patient?"** After the patient (or the decision maker for the patient) and the medical team agree on this goal, then the medical professionals can recommend ways to achieve that end. Here are the three possible goals of medical care:

1. **Cure.** Almost all healthcare today is focused on preventing and curing disease. We become sick. The physician prescribes a treatment. We hope to be cured.

2. **Stabilization of functioning.** Many diseases cannot be cured, but medical treatment can stabilize the patient and temporarily stop the disease from getting worse. For example, although there is no cure for diabetes, a person can take insulin injections for a lifetime and function fairly well. I have known several patients whose poorly functioning kidneys made it necessary for them to travel to a local

3

hospital three times a week for dialysis. These treatments can be considered appropriate even though they offer no hope of cure.

I also knew a 32-year-old man with muscular dystrophy. He breathed with the help of a mechanical ventilator and used a voice-activated computer. He was an avid sports fan and had a great sense of humor. This patient's treatment could not cure his disease, but he could function at a level acceptable to him.

3. **Preparing for a comfortable and dignified death.** This is the hospice care or "comfort measures only" approach. Each of the dialysis patients I mentioned before reached a point at which they decided that the treatment no longer offered them an acceptable quality of life, and so it was discontinued. They each died a short time later with appropriate care given to keep them comfortable.

Preparing for a comfortable and dignified death is a shift away from the direction of most medical care given today. It is a shift away from most of the medical training our physicians receive. It is also a shift away from the mission of our hospitals, which exist primarily to cure patients.

At times, these goals can be combined. I have seen many people decide to prepare for a comfortable and dignified death in the face of their end-stage cancer, but choose to cure pneumonia with antibiotics. Others in similar circumstances decline even the antibiotics.

Goals of care often change with the patient's condition. I asked the man on the ventilator under what condition he would like it turned off so that he might be allowed to die a natural death. He said, "When I end up like my roommate, who makes no response to anyone."

One way to find out if a treatment can accomplish a hoped-for outcome is to try it for a little while. Patients can try treatments in an effort to cure or stabilize, and then reassess after a certain period of time (see "A Time-Limited Trial," page 23).

During my first summer as a hospice chaplain, I was reminded once again of the importance of setting goals before deciding on treatment. We had admitted a new patient on a Friday. By the following Monday, I had two urgent voicemail messages from a nurse and a social worker. The messages went something like this: "Hank, we have a new patient who is very close to dying and her daughter wants everything done to try to save her, including CPR and ventilator support. Can you help?"

The patient was indeed very ill, and it turned out she was within a week of dying regardless of her treatment choices. She was totally dependent on her daughter for her care. She had just been discharged from the hospital after they were able to get her off of a ventilator. However, she still received her nutrition through a feeding tube.

When I got to the home, the patient was in a recliner in the middle of the family room. She could not speak nor lift a hand, although she did listen and seemed to understand what was going on. At the end of my visit, I asked the daughter to follow me out to the car so I could give her a copy of this book. I took the opportunity to try to convince her not to attempt heroic measures on her frail mother.

We spoke for a while, and soon, with tears running down her cheeks, she said, "All I want is for my mother to die peacefully here at home." I said, "We can help you with that, but it will not involve the rescue squad or putting your mother on machines."

I left. A few hours later, I received a call from the daughter. She had one question: "How long does it take a person to die if you stop tube feeding?" I told her what my experience had been, and assured her that her mother would be kept comfortable if she were to decide to stop the feedings.

I had not mentioned withdrawing the feeding tube. She had

*What really makes these decisions "hard choices" has little to do with the medical, legal, ethical, or moral aspects of the decision process. The real struggles are emotional and spiritual.*

already established the goal herself: "All I want is for my mother to die peacefully here at home." Once she had the goal in mind, the decision became more clear. She could then entertain the idea that perhaps a feeding tube is not compatible with a peaceful death. In the end, she did not have to decide. Her mother died peacefully at home three days later.

In my more than three decades as a chaplain at a nursing home, a hospice, and a hospital, I have been at the bedsides of many seriously ill patients. I have discussed these treatment choices with their families in the halls outside the patients' rooms. This first-hand experience adds as much value to the content of this book as the medical research upon which it is based.

I am convinced that what really makes these decisions "hard choices" has little to do with the medical, legal, ethical, or moral aspects of the decision process. The real struggles are emotional and spiritual. People wrestle with letting go and letting be. These are decisions of the heart, not just the head.

In Chapter Five of this book, I give my personal views on these decisions, especially on the spiritual and emotional struggles within (see page 54).

Citations for the research related to the topics discussed in this book are listed in the endnotes, pages 77–80. For a full listing of the endnotes and additional references, go to **www.hankdunn.com/references**.

# Chapter One:

## CPR—Cardiopulmonary Resuscitation

**This chapter will answer the following questions:**
- How successful are efforts to restart a heart?
- Can we know ahead of time which patients likely will not be revived by resuscitation efforts?
- How do patients let their wishes be known if they choose not to have resuscitation efforts?

During the 1960s, medical researchers developed a method of rescuing victims of sudden death. Known as cardiopulmonary resuscitation (CPR), this method is used when a person's heart and/or breathing stops. Traditionally, the rescuer repeatedly applies force to the victim's chest with the hands to compress the heart, and breathes into the patient's mouth to fill the lungs with air. These days, the rescue breaths are considered optional.[3] Thousands of lives are saved each year with CPR.

CPR was originally intended to be used for situations where death was accidental, such as drowning or electrical shock, or when an otherwise healthy person experienced a heart attack. Some of the early guidelines even said that there were certain cases when CPR should not be used: "**CPR is not indicated in certain situations, such as cases of terminal irreversible illness when death is not unexpected. . . . Resuscitation in these circumstances may represent a positive violation of a person's right to die with dignity.**"[4] Today, in hospitals, nursing homes, and residential care facilities, CPR has become standard practice on all patients who experience heart or breathing failure, except for those with orders restricting its use.

## Survival Rates with CPR

If a hospital patient's heart stops, a "code" is called and a special team responds. Treatment may include CPR, electrical shocks to the heart, injection of medications, and the use of a ventilator.

Approximately 17% of all hospital patients who receive CPR survive to be discharged.[5] Although it is hard to know exactly who will survive, we do know three categories of patients who most likely will NOT survive.

**Patients with the least chance of survival (usually less than 2% survive):**

- Those who have more than one or two serious medical conditions[6]
- Those who are dependent on others for their care or who live in a long-term care facility, like a nursing home[7]
- Those who have a terminal disease[6]

## The Burdens of CPR

Like most medical procedures, CPR has potential burdens. A frail patient may have their ribs broken or their lungs/spleen punctured because of the necessary force applied during CPR. If the patient has been without oxygen for too long, there will be brain damage if they are revived. This brain injury can range from subtle changes in intellect and personality all the way to permanent unconsciousness, called a "persistent vegetative state"[8] (see page 14).

Because of the chain of events put into motion when CPR is begun, a person could be placed on a breathing machine even though he or she might not have wanted it. For many patients, this risk of having severe brain injury and being "kept alive by machines" is a very serious burden. CPR also severely reduces the possibility of a peaceful death.

## CPR in Nursing Homes, Assisted Living, and Memory Care

Approximately 3% of nursing home residents whose heart or breathing stops receive resuscitation attempts.[9] Residential care homes have professionals on duty trained to administer CPR. If CPR is begun, the staff will call 911, and the rescue squad will arrive. Once on the scene, the paramedics take over the care of the resident. They will then continue CPR until the patient has been transported to the nearest emergency room, where the hospital staff will do everything in their power to bring the patient back to life. Measures could include continuing CPR, electrical shock, or the injection of medications. Once in the emergency room, patients may be connected to machines to keep them breathing through a tube inserted in the mouth and down the windpipe.

Calling 911 means that everything possible will be done to resuscitate the patient. It is good for us to know that the rescue squads in our communities will respond as quickly and as aggressively as possible to save lives. However, the research on CPR in nursing homes indicates that less than 2% of patients receiving resuscitation attempts survive.[7]

**Why does CPR offer so little hope of medical benefit for nursing home residents? Most of the characteristics that point to a poor prognosis for CPR survival are common in nursing home residents, who are often frail or debilitated.** By definition, residents do not live independently because of their generally failing health. Most also have multiple medical problems.

Some people ask, "Can we just try CPR at the residential care home and not transfer a resident to the emergency room for more aggressive treatment?" This is not standard procedure, and for good reason. The professionals at a care home want as much support as possible if they are trying to revive a resident. That support can come only from a rescue squad, and only the advanced medical team at an emergency room can determine whether all attempts at revival have failed.

Remember, once the chain of events is set in motion by beginning CPR, it is very difficult to stop until every procedure has been attempted. If CPR is successful, the patient will then need to stay in the hospital for follow-up care.

## CPR and the Patient with a Serious Illness

There are some patients who may benefit from CPR. An open, honest discussion with a physician will help any patient assess the possible benefit. But those who find themselves among the "patients with the least chance of survival" group will find the medical benefits from CPR are minimal.

Again, this would include patients with multiple serious medical problems, those who have a terminal disease, or those who are dependent on others for care, including long-term residents of nursing homes, assisted living facilities, and memory care facilities. In deciding whether to accept or reject CPR, one must weigh the facts. **Once a patient with one of the above conditions has a cardiac or respiratory arrest, there is only a small possibility of having the heart restarted. There is even less chance of surviving the subsequent hospitalization.**

*Because of the chain of events put into motion when CPR is begun, a person could be placed on a breathing machine even though he or she might not have wanted it.*

The frailty that goes with the worsened medical condition common among these patients contributes to this poor outlook for survival. Even if the patient survives the event that required CPR, the chances of long-term survival are slim. The individual's condition will most likely be much worse than before. Given these facts, many people choose not to have CPR used as a medical treatment for seriously ill patients. Others feel that CPR offers some hope of survival and that every effort should be made to save a person's life, no matter the medical condition or prognosis.

## CPR and Children

Some of the same conditions that make resuscitation attempts unsuccessful in the general population apply to children as well. Children with multiple organ system failure or those in the terminal phase of a disease have little chance of surviving CPR. What makes the decision to withhold resuscitation attempts on these little ones so difficult is the overwhelming sense of loss for the parents and for the medical staff.

Parents may feel like making the choice to say "do not resuscitate" symbolizes their lost hopes for the future of their child. The physician and other healthcare workers can help sort out the medical side of this decision. The more difficult part is letting go and letting be.

## CPR Is the Standard Order

Upon admission to a nursing home, an assisted living facility, memory care facility, or hospital, it is assumed that every patient whose heart stops will receive CPR. This presumption *for* CPR is reasonable, since any delay in beginning the procedure greatly reduces the chances for success.

This means that if a person would rather not have resuscitation attempts, a doctor must write an order restricting its use. This order goes by many different names: DNR (do not resuscitate), DNAR (do not attempt resuscitation), AND (allow natural death), No Code, or No CPR. This order must be given by the physician, and often the family or the patient must request it. In most cases, the staff or physician will not make a DNR decision without a discussion with the patient or family, no matter how seriously ill a patient may be.

Also keep in mind that when 911 is called, the rescue squad

will automatically attempt CPR on any person whose heart or breathing stops. Many states provide a document or bracelet to show the emergency personnel if the patient would not want to receive resuscitation attempts. Sometimes called an "Out-of-Hospital DNR Order," this document can allow a family to feel confident in calling the rescue squad for help. They can know they will receive comfort care and supportive help for the patient while not running the risk of attempts at resuscitation or being "hooked up to machines."

**Chapter One Summary:**

- About 17% of patients in hospitals who have undergone CPR survive to be discharged.

- In most cases, patients with multiple serious medical problems, with a terminal illness, or who cannot live independently survive CPR less than 2% of the time.

- Possible burdens of "successful" CPR include fractured ribs, punctured lungs, brain damage, depression, never regaining consciousness, risk of the patient being connected to machines for his or her remaining days, and reduced possibility of a peaceful death.

- Patients, or those making decisions for them, may request from the physician an order not to attempt resuscitation.

# Chapter Two:

## Feeding Tubes—Artificial Nutrition and Hydration

**This chapter will answer the following questions:**

- What are some of the benefits and hazards of using feeding tubes?
- What are some of the advantages of dying without the use of artificial feeding or IVs?
- What is a time-limited trial?

When a patient can no longer take food or fluid by mouth, a feeding tube can sometimes be used instead. Liquid nutritional supplements, water, and medications can be poured into the tube or pumped in by way of a mechanical device. Tubes usually come in one of two types:

- **The nasogastric (NG) tube** is inserted through the nose, down the esophagus, and into the stomach.

- **The gastrostomy** is a tube inserted surgically through the skin into the stomach wall. Sometimes this method is called a PEG* tube, or a G-tube.

There are other types of tubes, such as jejunal tubes (J-tubes). These tubes bypass the stomach and are inserted directly into the small intestine. There is also the less common TPN**, when a catheter or needle is inserted in a vein, often in the chest, and a liquid containing nutrients is pumped directly into the blood stream, bypassing the entire digestive system.

---

\*  Percutaneous endoscopic gastrostomy
\*\*Total parenteral nutrition

## The Benefits of Artificial Feeding

Feeding tubes have proved beneficial to thousands of patients. Many people, such as some stroke patients, need the help of a feeding tube for a short period before going back to eating by mouth. Others live with a gastrostomy tube and enjoy reading, watching television, visiting with their families, and other activities.

One patient I visited had a feeding tube because he lost the ability to swallow due to throat cancer. He lived alone and was hampered in his ability to care for himself because of emphysema. I asked him once how he felt about the feeding tube. "Great!" he said. "I don't have to go grocery shopping. I don't have any pots and pans to wash. And I can stay in my own home." Clearly he felt he benefited from the feeding tube.

## Artificial Feeding in Non-Responsive Patients

**Often a patient with a serious or long-term chronic illness never regains the ability to eat or drink.** Some people survive for years on a feeding tube. Karen Ann Quinlan, although disconnected from a respirator, lived unconscious for more than 10 years receiving nutrition and hydration through a feeding tube. In another well-known case, Rita Greene, who made no response to any stimuli, lived for 48 years with the aid of a feeding tube.

Patients who make no purposeful response to their surroundings have been described as either permanently unconscious or in a persistent vegetative state (PVS).[10] Most often these patients suffered brain damage from an interruption of the flow of blood to the brain. All their vital body functions operate without the aid of machinery with only the artificially supplied nutrition and hydration needed to keep them alive. Frequently they are young people left in this condition after an automobile or sporting accident. Sometimes, people end up in this non-responsive condition after "successful" CPR.

As one might expect, a variety of opinions are expressed about whether or not to artificially feed and/or hydrate hopelessly ill or dying patients. There is a wealth of research and opinions on the use of artificial nutrition and hydration with the goal of discovering whether or not using it is helpful to the patient or whether it does harm. Often the standard medical practice is to start tube feeding for any patient who can no longer take in enough food or water by mouth. A patient may receive a feeding tube unless the patient or family makes a conscious choice not to do so.

## The Burdens of Artificial Feeding

Feeding tubes are not without risk. Pneumonia can develop if the tube becomes displaced or if vomit enters the lungs.[11] Ulcers and infections can also result from a feeding tube.[12] A patient who repeatedly removes the tube will probably need to be restrained or sedated. The immobility of most of these patients makes them prime candidates for bedsores and stiff limbs.[13] Furthermore, patients can be more isolated with artificial feeding than hand feeding because they lose the personal interaction of someone sitting with them and feeding them three times a day.

A stroke patient with an artificial feeding tube came to our nursing home from the hospital. She made little response to caregivers and to her family. The family had agreed they would try the feeding tube for a year, and if there were no improvement, they would stop the treatment and let her die.

At the end of the year, along with withdrawing the artificial feeding, a speech therapist worked with the patient to try to help her eat again by mouth. Not only did she live for another year without the artificial feeding, but her whole personality changed. She was more interactive, smiled more, and generally seemed to be in better health. I was able to observe this patient with and without artificial feeding, and the difference was striking. I know this is just one case, but I am convinced that the personal connection with the nurse or aide three times daily, plus the pleasurable stimulation of eating, changed this woman's life.

## The Case for Artificial Feeding in Most Circumstances

Some say that a feeding tube should be used in most cases because food and water are forms of basic care that should not be denied to anyone, no matter what their prognosis is for recovery. They might also say that feeding tubes should be used in most cases because they feel the benefits outweigh the burdens. Those who advocate such a position often allow that an adult who is able to make decisions can refuse any medical treatment, including artificial nutrition and hydration.

Those who advocate for using a feeding tube under most circumstances might characterize the act of not providing nutrition and hydration artificially as "starvation." Indeed, anyone who does not receive food and water will die, although their condition would more accurately be described as "dehydrated" rather than "malnourished"[14] (see pages 18–19).

They also might describe the insertion of a feeding tube as just providing "basic food and water" like hand feeding and, therefore, not a medical intervention.[15] Additionally, since the patient will die in a short time if a feeding tube is removed, they may argue that the intent of those removing the tube is to end the life of the patient, which is clearly against the very nature of medicine.[16]

## The Case against Artificial Feeding in Some Circumstances

Many people feel that the use of feeding tubes in some cases may cause excessive burdens in the patient or may provide insufficient benefits, and therefore they are not obligated to use them in all cases. They might make the argument that artificial feeding of terminally ill persons or those in an irreversible coma is more of a burden than a benefit to the patient.

We are not obligated to preserve our lives at all costs. People who choose not to have life prolonged on a mechanical ventilator are, in a way, "denied" air. Some consider withholding or withdrawing feeding tubes to be similar to taking someone off of a ventilator. Feeding tubes become morally optional when they are no longer beneficial for the patient or would cause clinical burdens or significant physical discomfort.

People who advocate the removal of feeding tubes in some circumstances might see the inability to take in food and water by mouth as a terminal medical condition. To withhold or withdraw artificial feeding is to let death from the underlying condition occur naturally.[14] **When a person dies after the withholding of artificial food and fluids, the death is from the condition or disease that made the patient unable to eat, not from the removal of artificial feeding.** Therefore, nothing is being introduced to "kill" the patient, but the natural process of dying is being allowed to progress.[17] Choosing not to force-feed a person is choosing not to prolong the dying process.

Common medical practice says that a doctor can ethically withdraw all means of life-prolonging medical treatment, including food and water, from a patient in an irreversible coma. Courts in many states and the U.S. Supreme Court have upheld this view and allowed the withdrawal of feeding tubes. There is a consensus among state legislatures and in medical literature viewing artificial feeding as a medical procedure that may be withdrawn.[18]

### *Intravenous (IV) Artificial Hydration*

A common method of artificial hydration, especially in a hospital, is the IV line. A patient can receive fluids and medications through a needle or catheter (plastic tube) in the arm. The process of inserting the IV can be uncomfortable. The patient may need to have the point of insertion changed frequently if the IV does not work, or every three to five days to prevent infection or irritation. If patients pull at the tubes, their hands may need to be tied down. For most patients, these are appropriate and acceptable burdens.

Although this chapter mostly addresses the use of feeding tubes, IVs are related. When used to hydrate a dying patient, IVs are included in the discussion of feeding tubes because they also supply hydration artificially. Patients and families should frequently reconsider whether the use of IVs is appropriate, especially as the time of death approaches. Much of what we know about withholding artificial hydration at the end of life has been discovered as caregivers observed patients dying with and without the use of IV fluids.

> **The benefits of NOT using artificial hydration (via an IV or a feeding tube) in a dying patient:**
> - Less fluid congesting the lungs, making breathing easier
> - Less fluid in the throat and less need for suctioning
> - Less pressure around tumors and less pain
> - Less urination, less need to move the patient to change the bed linens, and less risk of bedsores
> - Less fluid retained in the patient's hands, feet, and body (forcing liquids into a person whose body is shutting down can create an uncomfortable buildup of fluid)
> - Natural pain-relieving chemicals are released as the body dehydrates, causing a sense of well-being sometimes described as "mild euphoria" (this state also suppresses the appetite)[19]

## Does Withholding or Withdrawing Artificial Feeding Cause a Painful Death?

To say that withholding or withdrawing artificial nutrition and hydration is "starvation" (and therefore perhaps causing suffering) is inaccurate. Whatever pain or discomfort is associated with malnutrition (i.e., starvation) is not relevant here, because a patient will be affected by dehydration long before suffering any ill effects from the lack of nutritional support.[14]

Therefore, pain treatments must address any pain a dehydrating patient may suffer as well as addressing the relief of acute pain that may be the result of another condition, such as cancer. A genuine concern on everyone's part is pain control. If a patient is allowed to die by forgoing artificial feeding, can pain and discomfort be held to a minimum? The answer is "yes."

Patients who have had brain damage and no longer respond to their environment "cannot experience pain and suffering."[10] For patients who have some responses, there are ways to alleviate acute pain without the use of artificial feeding tubes or IV hydration.

Beyond the issue of acute pain is the question of whether dying of dehydration causes any other unnecessary pain or unusual suffering. **The medical evidence is quite clear that dehydration in the end stage of a terminal illness is a very natural and compassionate way to die.**[20]

**The only uncomfortable symptoms of dehydration are a dry mouth and a sense of thirst,** both of which can be alleviated with good mouth care and ice chips or sips of water but are not necessarily relieved by artificial hydration.

No matter what the treatment choice regarding feeding tubes, **comfort care and freedom from pain are essential goals of any medical team.** Just because extraordinary or heroic measures have been withheld or withdrawn does not mean that routine nursing care and comfort care are withheld. A patient will always receive pain medication, oxygen, or any other treatment deemed necessary to ensure as much comfort as possible.

## *The Difference Between Withholding and Withdrawing*

Imagine how emotionally difficult it would be to withdraw a feeding tube from a person who has been kept alive through artificial means for several months or years. For a family and physician to change the treatment plan like this requires a change in perspective. A person has been living with a feeding tube and now the decision has been made to allow that person to die. It is not impossible, emotionally, to come to this point of withdrawing treatment, but it is more difficult than withholding the artificial feeding in the first place.

**From moral, ethical, medical, and most religious viewpoints there is no difference between withholding and withdrawing. Emotionally, there is a world of difference.** And as much as we might like to think physicians do not make decisions and recommendations based on emotion, it is just as difficult for them to suggest or accept a change from using the tube to withdrawing.

A family I once knew wanted to withdraw artificial feeding from the patient, and the physician told me, "I would have had no problem not starting the treatment in the first place but I cannot order the withdrawal." There is nothing in law, medicine, ethics, or morality to justify such a stance. If withholding treatment would have been acceptable earlier, then only emotion could now require its continuation.[21]

The difficulty of making the decision to withdraw treatment makes it very important to think through and discuss these issues long before a crisis comes. **If a patient or family does not want to use artificial feeding, it is much better not to begin the feeding at all. But if it is begun, artificial feeding can be withdrawn at a later date.**

### Artificial Feeding and the Dementia Patient

**Alzheimer's disease and other forms of dementia are characterized by the deterioration of the person over a number of years.** In earlier stages of the disease, it may be helpful to the patient to use a feeding tube as a temporary measure in the event of a decline in appetite or weight loss. The hope is that the patient will eventually be able to take in enough food and fluid by mouth to be able to discontinue the tube.

In advanced dementia, research has shown that a feeding tube does not offer benefit to the patient, even with temporary use.[22] **Dementia is a terminal disease.** Like all terminal conditions, dementia has symptoms that indicate when the end of the disease process may be near.

> **The signs of the end stage of Alzheimer's and other dementias are well documented:**[23]
>
> - Incontinence
> - Progressive loss of speech
> - Loss of intentional movement
> - Complete dependence for dressing, eating, and toileting
> - Inability to recognize loved ones
> - Eating difficulties, possibly including the loss of the ability to swallow

One of the symptoms in the terminal phase of this disease—swallowing difficulty—has sometimes been treated with feeding tubes. **The truth is artificial feeding does not lengthen the life of an end-stage dementia patient and only adds greater burdens.**[24]

A main hazard of hand feeding a dementia patient is the possibility of the patient getting food in the lungs, which could cause aspiration pneumonia. Some would rather start an artificial feeding tube to avoid the difficulties of hand feeding while hoping to reduce the possibility of causing pneumonia. However, the risk of aspiration is not eliminated by tube feedings, either. Some research indicates that pneumonia is a greater risk with a feeding tube.[21] Careful hand feeding (for example, keeping the head of the bed elevated and using soft foods) can reduce, though not eliminate, this risk.

Many healthcare professionals feel that because the feeding tube does not lengthen the life of the patient and causes greater burdens, careful hand feeding should be used instead.[11] Although pneumonia is a risk, those who would forgo the feeding tube view it as an acceptable risk. **They see the swallowing difficulties as part of the end of a very tragic disease process and know that introducing artificial feeding does not cure the underlying affliction—dementia.**

Numerous medical studies have found that tube feeding of advanced dementia patients offers absolutely no benefit and even causes some harm. In one such study, the researchers concluded, "We identified no direct data to support tube feeding of demented patients with eating difficulties for any of the commonly cited indications." Several more recent studies have come to similar conclusions.[25]

> **The facts about tube feeding for advanced dementia patients (like end-stage Alzheimer's):**
> - Tube feeding is a risk factor for aspiration pneumonia.
> - Survival has not been shown to be prolonged by tube feeding.
> - Tube-fed patients are more likely to develop pressure sores (bedsores).
> - Delivery of nutrients via tube has not been shown to reduce infection; on the contrary, feeding tubes have been shown to cause serious local and systemic infection.
> - These patients are uncomfortable from tube feeding and may need to be restrained to avoid pulling the tube out.
> - Functional status has not been shown to improve, while dozens of serious adverse effects have been reported.[25]

Inserting a feeding tube in an advanced dementia patient is a treatment to question, according to two physician professional societies. "Choosing Wisely" asked 70 medical societies to list "Things Providers and Patients Should Question." The American Academy of Hospice and Palliative Medicine and the American Geriatrics Society agreed on questioning feeding tubes for Alzheimer's patients. These two groups, independently, listed the use of feeding tubes in advanced dementia patients as the number one treatment to avoid. Visit **www.choosingwisely.org** for more information.

## Artificial Feeding and Children

As difficult as it may be to withhold or withdraw artificial feeding from a failing 80-year-old patient, it only gets harder in making a decision like this for a child. When elderly patients stop eating, we can usually accept that as a sign that they are nearing the end of life. But a child is just beginning life. The medical realities may be no different between the seriously ill child and the adult, but it *feels* different.

We would not expect young children or infants to be able to feed themselves even if they were healthy. So artificial nutrition and hydration might be seen as just another way of helping them "eat." Parents seek to feed their children from the first hours of life. These instincts are difficult to overcome as one considers refusing artificial feeding.

Again, as with CPR, the grief issues are great. We face losing our child, our child's future, our future, our hopes—all difficult things to go through.

## A Time-Limited Trial

Patients who are having eating difficulties (or their designated decision makers) can consider a few different treatment options: to use feeding tubes, to withhold or withdraw them, or to use a compromise treatment plan.

One compromise option is a time-limited trial of a feeding tube.[26] To do this, secure an agreement with the attending physician to try artificial feeding for a limited time. If there is little or no improvement in the patient at the end of the trial, or if there is no possibility of the patient regaining consciousness or the ability to swallow, then the artificial feeding may be withdrawn at that point. **Another compromise is using artificial feeding to supplement hand feeding.** I know some patients who eat what they can during the day and have a feeding tube running at night.

If the patient cannot make the decision, the family will have to decide on behalf of the patient. They will have to live with their decision, which may be a difficult burden to carry. I am convinced that this burden is heavy because of the emotional/spiritual struggle of the family to let go.

Medicine, law, ethics, and morality all are affected by this emotional struggle. No matter whether you choose a feeding tube or not in your particular case, you can find plenty of company. Religious leaders, ethicists, politicians, nurses, and physicians are divided on this topic. It is understandable that people grapple with this issue. We are letting go of someone important to us. Even when it makes perfect sense to withhold or withdraw artificial feeding from a medical viewpoint, it can still be hard. I discuss this emotional and spiritual struggle in more detail in the final chapter.

**Chapter Two Summary:**

- Feeding tubes can help many patients get through temporary times of eating difficulties. Other patients choose to use one permanently after they have lost the ability to swallow.

- Permanently unconscious patients can be maintained for years with a feeding tube, but people disagree whether such treatment should be withdrawn.

- Patients with advanced dementia (like end-stage Alzheimer's disease) will not be helped with the use of artificial feeding tubes, and may actually be harmed.

- A time-limited trial can be used to try a treatment for a period of time, and, if it does not help the patient, then it can be discontinued.

- Dying patients are much more comfortable without the use of artificial hydration, whether provided by feeding tubes or IVs.

# Chapter Three:

## Cure Sometimes, Comfort Always

*L*iving with a serious illness may involve experiencing pain and other uncomfortable symptoms. Fortunately, medical interventions can reduce pain and other burdens brought on by disease. We do not have to just endure.

Comfort care—commonly provided by palliative care services or hospice programs—seeks to make the patient more comfortable in spite of serious illness, while also addressing the needs of the family. Palliative and hospice care are each used in a different circumstance:

**Palliative care** is for anybody with a serious illness. You can receive it at any point of an illness, and you can have it along with curative treatment. Eligibility is not dependent on prognosis or age.

**Hospice care** is an important benefit that provides palliative care for terminally ill patients who may have only months to live. People who choose hospice also want their treatment to focus on their comfort but are no longer receiving curative treatment for their underlying disease.

Though hospice and palliative care are widely available, some communities may not yet have programs in place. Even so, a patient can still receive comfort measures. These approaches are just good, compassionate, and

*Comfort care seeks to make the patient more comfortable in spite of serious illness, while also addressing the needs of the family.*

comprehensive medical care. If separate hospice or palliative care services are not accessible, talk to your doctor about how to receive this type of care.

## Palliative Care

**This section will answer the following questions:**
- What is palliative care?
- Can I still pursue a cure to my disease while receiving palliative care?
- What does palliative care do?

Palliative care is specialized medical care for those with serious or chronic illnesses, including cancer, cardiac disease, COPD (chronic obstructive pulmonary disease), kidney failure, Alzheimer's, Parkinson's, ALS (amyotrophic lateral sclerosis/Lou Gehrig's disease), and many more.

This kind of care focuses on providing patients with relief from the symptoms and stress of their sickness. It is appropriate at any age and at any stage in a serious illness. The goal is to improve quality of life for both the patient and the family.

A question often asked is, "Can I have treatment to cure my disease together with palliative care?" The answer is, "Absolutely." Treatment choices are up to the patient. Palliative care can be given at the same time as curative treatment.

In fact, palliative care can often improve a patient's ability to tolerate medical treatments, giving them strength to carry on with daily life. It gives patients more control over their care by helping them understand their choices for treatment.

Most of the text in this section is provided with permission from the Center to Advance Palliative Care (CAPC). Visit their website for more information: **www.getpalliativecare.org.**

## A Partnership of Patient, Specialists, and Family

Palliative care is a team approach to care. The core team includes specially trained palliative care doctors, nurses, and social workers. Massage therapists, physical and occupational therapists, pharmacists, nutritionists, chaplains, and others may also be part of the team.

The palliative care team members partner with the patient, the family, and the patient's other doctors to provide an extra layer of support. They spend as much time as necessary with the patient and family, supporting them every step of the way. The care team not only focuses on keeping the patient's symptoms under control, but also helps the patient and family to understand the treatment options and achieve their goals of care.

## What to Expect from Palliative Care

- **Pain and symptom control.** The palliative care team will identify sources of pain and discomfort. These may include problems with nausea, loss of appetite, shortness of breath, fatigue, depression, anxiety, insomnia, or the bowel or bladder. Then the team will provide treatments that can offer relief. These might include medication along with massage therapy or relaxation techniques.

- **Communication and coordination.** Palliative care teams put great importance on communication between the patient, the family, and physicians in order to ensure that the needs of the patient and family are fully met. These needs often include establishing goals of care, help with decision making, and coordination of care.

- **Emotional support.** Palliative care focuses on the entire person, not just the illness. The team members will address any social, psychological, emotional, or spiritual needs the patient may have.

- **Family/caregiver support.** Caregivers bear a great deal of stress, so the palliative care team supports them as well. This focused attention helps ease some of the strain and can help patients and families with decision making.

## Hospice Care

**This section will answer the following questions:**
- What is hospice?
- When is the right time to "prepare for dying"?
- How can I try to ensure that there will be a peaceful death?
- What is appropriate care for end-stage dementia patients?

### What Is Hospice?

How do we know if a medical procedure offers promise of cure or freedom from pain, or if it is making the dying process unnatural and burdensome? How can we prepare for the death of someone we love and make the experience as meaningful and as painless as possible?

The hospice movement has led the way in answering these questions. It has taught us that letting someone die naturally does not mean we stop treating or caring for them. **At the center of hospice care is the belief that each of us has the right to die without pain and with dignity, and that our families will receive the necessary support to allow us to do so.**

The term "hospice" (from the same linguistic root as "hospitality") can be traced back to early Western civilization. It was used then to describe a place of shelter and rest for weary or sick travelers on long journeys. The term was first applied to specialized care for dying patients in 1967 at St. Christopher's Hospice in a residential suburb of London.

**Hospice provides the same valuable services as palliative**

care, including pain and symptom control, communication and coordination, emotional support, and family/caregiver support (see page 27–28).

The difference between hospice and palliative care is that hospice focuses solely on comfort measures for those in the last phase of life. In most cases, care is provided in the patient's home, but it is also provided in freestanding hospice houses, hospitals, nursing homes, and other long-term care facilities like assisted living or memory care units.

Hospice, just like palliative care, is a team approach to care. Hospice provides a team of professionals and specially trained volunteers to address the medical, social, psychological, and spiritual needs of the patient and the family, wherever the patient resides. If the choice is made to stay at home, the hospice team is accessible around the clock for support, consultation, and visits.

In a hospital or nursing home, the team becomes an adjunct to the staff in advising, teaching, observing, and supporting the patient and family, and provides extra equipment if it is needed. Inpatient hospice facilities incorporate the whole hospice philosophy in a unique, comforting setting (such as a free-standing hospice house) with specially trained staff.

*Wherever hospice services are given, emphasis is on management of pain and other symptoms. Quality of life is the focus, rather than length of life.*

Wherever hospice services are given, the emphasis is on management of pain and other symptoms. Quality of life is the focus, rather than length of life. Surprisingly, research has found that patients receiving hospice care may actually live longer, even when they have stopped curative treatment.[27] Hospice care continues after a patient's death with grief counseling services for families and friends of the patient.

Although enrolling in hospice offers the most comprehensive benefits to patients and families, the hospice philosophy of care can be reflected by a physician's order called "comfort measures only." To understand the meaning of this approach, it is helpful to review the goals of medical treatment.

## Goals of Medical Treatment in the "Last Phase of Life"

Up until the second half of the 20th century, our final illness was usually short-lived, and it was clear that the patient would die within the foreseeable future. Now, most of us will die of chronic diseases such as heart disease, cancer, stroke, or dementia. We will probably live with these diseases for years before dying of them. We may have times of being very close to death, only to then recover and live for months or even years.[28] It's no wonder why we have difficulty today answering the question, "When am I dying?"

In my work as a healthcare chaplain, I have helped patients and families answer that question. Rather than talking to families about "dying" I might ask, "Would you say your mother is in the last phase of her life?" For seriously ill patients, most people are comfortable referring to the illness as part of the "last phase" even though they may not say "dying." We usually reserve the term "dying" for the last days or hours of a person's life.

A method physicians often use to identify when a patient is dying is called the "surprise question." They ask themselves, "Would I be surprised if the patient died in the next year?" If the answer is "no," then the patient is clearly in the last phase of life.[29]

In the Introduction, I describe **the three possible goals of medical care as cure, stabilization of functioning, and preparing for a comfortable and dignified death** (see pages 3–4). Clearly, when we know a person has reached the final days or hours of life, almost all of us would choose preparing for a comfortable and dignified death. Equally clear, when we are healthy and have no other medical problems, we would usually choose to cure an illness.

What about the last phase of life as we live with a long-term chronic illness? Well, sometimes we choose "cure" and sometimes "preparing for death." I have seen many patients with congestive heart failure suffer a life-threatening episode before being rushed to the hospital for aggressive curative treatment. Sometimes, those patients are back at home the very next day resuming their usual activities.

So it is appropriate, in some cases, for heart patients to be hospitalized. But some of these patients get to the point when they or their family decide "no more hospitals." Fortunately, good medical care, such as hospice care, can offer an acceptable quality of life in the home even when the disease cannot be cured.

At any point during a long-term chronic illness (like heart failure, Alzheimer's, or respiratory failure), or during a more short-term illness (like some cancers), patients and families need to prepare emotionally and spiritually for the possibility of death. This preparation can be done even while trying to cure the disease that could bring death at any time. All during the course of the illness, patients and families need to weigh the benefits of treatment with the quality of life.

If quality of life diminishes, some patients may choose to stop some treatment to preserve quality. When aggressive treatment no longer benefits a patient, the choice may be made to prepare for a comfortable and dignified death.

If asked, most people say, "I want to die peacefully in my sleep in my own bed." A few people have told me, "I would like to die in a hospital." The hope is that the patient's preference can be honored. For those who would like to die peacefully wherever they call home, hospice may be a good option.

## What Are Comfort Measures?

Some treatments are intended only to provide comfort to a patient and not prolong the dying process. For example, medicines that reduce fever or pain are comfort measures. Oxygen can be used to make breathing easier. Routine nursing care, such as keeping the patient clean and changing linens, adds to the comfort of the one who is dying. Emotional and spiritual support, both to the patient and the family, are provided by staff members, chaplains, and volunteers. Choosing hospice or comfort measures only does not mean care or treatment stops. **"Cure sometimes, comfort always" is a constant reminder of the goals of this approach.**

## *Which Medical Treatments Are Optional?*

With a hospice (or comfort measures only) approach, some treatments might be withheld or withdrawn:

- Usually a cancer patient would no longer receive radiation or chemotherapy to cure the disease, but these treatments might be used to relieve pain.

- Antibiotics may not routinely be used to treat an infection like pneumonia, but the patient may choose to seek a cure from it. Again, antibiotics may be used if necessary to relieve pain (see page 43).

- Most diagnostic tests may be eliminated, especially testing that might involve painful procedures like drawing blood. If there will no longer be active treatment to cure the patient, then diagnostic testing is not needed.

- A feeding tube would not routinely be started. If one is already in place, then withdrawal of the tube could be considered separate from the "comfort measures only" order. Remember, artificial nutrition and hydration may only add to the discomfort of the dying patient. Likewise, IVs might be used as a means of infusing pain medication but usually not for hydration.

- Usually surgery would not be performed unless it was deemed necessary to promote the comfort of the patient.

## Which Patients Are Candidates for Comfort Measures Only? When Is the Right Time?

Hospice care is used for those with a life-limiting progressive illness with six months or less to live if the disease runs its normal course. Often, but not always, hospice patients know that cure is impossible. They wish for a high quality of life for however long they have left.

**Early admission into hospice allows more time for the hospice team to fully understand the needs of the patient and family, and to develop a suitable plan of care.** Perhaps most important of all, if a relationship of trust between the patient and the hospice team can develop over several months, the patient can enjoy the full benefit of hospice care. Families report better end-of-life care experiences when they start hospice care earlier.[30]

Any person who is in the end stage of any disease process would be a candidate for a comfort measures only order and certainly for hospice. Of course, a patient with the capacity to make decisions may refuse any treatment with a goal of cure or stabilization and request a comfort measures only order. Physicians and nurses can provide guidance to determine when a patient is probably in the end stage of a disease.

This shift from a goal of "cure" to one of "preparing for a comfortable death" often comes gradually over time. It does not happen suddenly one day. Most of us would like to live as well as possible for as long as possible, even with a serious disease. During the course of the illness we can always prepare for the eventuality of our own death.

Toward the end stages of any disease, more emphasis is placed on the comfort of the patient as opposed to curing the disease. We can come to the point of doing nothing, or very little, to extend the life of the patient. Usually we know the "time is right" when:

- Death is a strong probability

- Available treatments will likely extend pain and suffering
- Successful treatment is more likely to bring extended unconsciousness or advanced dementia than cure
- Available treatments increase the probability of a death "hooked up to machines" when the patient would have preferred otherwise[31]

## End-Stage Dementia (like Alzheimer's) and Comfort Measures Only

A patient who does not have decision-making capacity and has left no instructions about the appropriate time to refuse curative treatment should be provided reasonable curative care as long as it is not the end stage of a disease process. When the patient is in the end stage of Alzheimer's or other forms of dementia, focusing on comfort measures only is the more appropriate treatment goal.

Many hospice patients are those who have been diagnosed with cancer. **Yet more and more patients suffering from dementia and other chronic diseases are entering hospice care or receiving a comfort measures only treatment plan.**[32] Because of the terminal nature of dementia and the clear signs of the approach of the end stage (see page 21), many advocate that families consider comfort measures only (i.e., a hospice treatment plan) for these patients.

## Children and Comfort Measures Only

Parents just assume that they will die before their children. I have seen agonizing grief from someone in her 80s who lost a 65-year-old child. It wasn't meant to be that way. And when a child is school age or younger, the unfairness seems more profound.

Yet the harsh reality is that some children do die. Although none of us would ever want to lose a child, if it were going to happen, we would want them to have as peaceful a passing as possible. This takes planning and preparation. The first step toward a comfortable and dignified death is accepting the terminal diagnosis. An earlier recognition of the prognosis contributes to a more peaceful death.[33]

When should children be involved in their own medical treatment decisions, especially as it relates to withholding or withdrawing life-sustaining care? They, of course, would have to have the maturity to understand their disease, prognosis, and what treatment options are available to them. Adolescents' opinions should be considered.[34] Other children could participate according to their abilities. The American Academy of Pediatrics believes that the views of even very young children should be factored into the end-of-life decision-making process.[35]

The emotional and spiritual struggles are the most difficult. It is hard to let go of a child. I once had a 14-year-old patient who lived with his mother. He had a cancer that had filled his chest and arms with tumors. Breathing was so difficult that the most comfortable position for him was to sit on the side of the bed and lean over on a pillow on a tray table. Sometimes he sat like this day and night.

His mother said she wanted everything done to save her son's life, including CPR and mechanical ventilators. One day we talked about her pursuing such aggressive treatment. She was very religious and said, "I figure if I call 911 and he ends up on machines at the hospital, it's God's will. And if I don't call and he dies peacefully here at home, it's God's will."

Remembering my principle of establishing a goal first, I said, "What could you imagine as the most peaceful death your son could have?" She said, "I have thought a lot about that, and I just hope one morning I come into his room and find that he died in his sleep." I told her, "The death hooked up to machines is the accident. A peaceful death in his own bed takes planning."

That night, after his father visited, the child relaxed for the first time in days and lay down on the bed. His mother climbed into bed with him. Before long, his breathing stopped. His peaceful death came in his mother's arms. She was able to let go and let be.

## *Turning from Cure to Comfort Measures Only*

**Patients and families can find great healing when it is time to move away from efforts to cure the disease toward more reasonable and meaningful goals.** The alleviation of pain, reconciliation, healing of broken relationships, finding deeper spiritual values, laughing about old times while celebrating the life of the patient, sharing the patient's grief and anger, and saying goodbye are all reasonable hopes for the last days and months of any of our lives. To continue to fight for a cure when there is no reasonable hope for one may cut off the true growth and comfort that can come from going on this journey together with those we love.

### Chapter Three Summary:

- Palliative care is for anyone with a serious illness. A patient can receive it at any age and any stage of an illness.

- Palliative care focuses on providing patients with relief from the symptoms and stress of a serious illness. The goal is to improve quality of life for both the patient and the family.

- A patient can be in a palliative care program and still receive treatment to try to cure a disease.

- During the last phase of life, a time will likely come when the focus shifts from "cure" to "comfort measures only" and/ or to enter hospice.

- Hospice is a medical care program designed to keep terminally ill patients free of pain while paying special attention to the emotional and spiritual needs of both the patient and the family.

- Dying in the hospital ICU hooked up to machines and tubes is the accident. A peaceful death in one's own bed takes planning.

- When advanced dementia reaches the end stage, it may be appropriate to shift to comfort measures only or hospice.

# Chapter Four:

## Treatments to Consider—Practical Help for Decision Making

**This chapter will answer the following questions:**

- What are the issues one needs to consider when thinking about hospitalization, ventilator support, dialysis, the use of antibiotics, or pacemakers or implanted defibrillators?

- How do I communicate my treatment wishes to the medical team caring for me?

- What is an advance directive? What is the difference between a living will and a durable power of attorney for healthcare? What is a POLST form?

- What are some questions that need to be answered to help make a decision about life-prolonging procedures?

### *Treatment Option: Hospitalization*

This is the last of the four most common treatment decisions you might face.* If patients living at home or in a residential care facility experience a sudden decline in their health, often they are transferred to a hospital in an effort to make them better. Sometimes even patients who want no heroic measures can benefit from hospital admission to get symptoms under control or to treat a special need, like a hip fracture. When considering going into a hospital, one must weigh the burdens as well as the possible benefits.

---

\* The four most common decisions concern CPR, artificial nutrition and hydration, hospitalization, and the hospice approach (see page 2).

**The burdens of hospitalization include:**

- Increased possibility of anxiety while getting used to new surroundings, new caregivers, and new routines (this is especially difficult for dementia patients)[36]
- Increased possibility of contracting an infection
- Increased possibility of the use of restraints or sedation, especially for dementia patients
- Increased possibility of aggressively treating any condition because that is the ordinary practice in the hospital
- Increased possibility of diagnostic testing that may be burdensome or painful, especially if the patient or family already knows they would not seek treatment for any disease the tests might reveal

If the patient can receive the same type of care (for example, IV antibiotics) in their normal residence, one might ask: "Why transfer to the hospital?" In the rare case when pain can be controlled only in the hospital, hospitalization would be appropriate. Of course, some patients prefer being in the hospital because they feel they get better care. Patient and family preference is the primary concern.

One treatment option to reduce the aggressiveness of medical care is the DNH (Do Not Hospitalize) order. Some facilities call this "Do Not Transport" to the hospital. **The essential question here is: "Can comfort care, pain control, and any desired and appropriate treatment seeking to cure be provided in the patient's place of residence?" If the answer is "yes," then a DNH order might be appropriate for the patient.**

The DNH order is especially helpful if a patient has a change in condition and the attending physician cannot be contacted. The physician on call may have no prior knowledge of the patient's history or of the wishes of the patient/family in regard to how aggressively to treat the patient. The DNH order helps the physician and staff know about this treatment choice if the family or attending physician cannot be contacted immediately. The DNH order does *not* mean that the patient can *never* be hospitalized, but only that the patient will not be hospitalized without a thorough discussion with the patient (if he or she is able to make decisions), the family, and the attending physician.

## *Treatment Option: Ventilators (Breathing Machines)*

When a person's breathing fails, a machine may be used to aid the patient. This machine is called a ventilator or respirator. Ventilators are commonly used to support respiratory function during and after anesthesia for major operations. Sometimes they may help a patient with a severe illness such as stroke, pneumonia, or heart failure.

When a ventilator is used, the machine is connected to a tube that is inserted through the mouth and down the windpipe, allowing the machine to force air into the lungs. Sometimes the tube is surgically connected through the throat and directly into the windpipe. This surgical connection is called a "tracheostomy" or "trach."

The tube is uncomfortable, and sometimes a patient needs to be tied down or sedated to prevent pulling at the tube, which could dislodge it and cause harm. This discomfort is acceptable to most people, because the tube and ventilator are removed as soon as the need for them is gone.

But some patients who have a long history of a disease that causes respiratory failure (like COPD*, emphysema, or heart failure) or neurologic diseases (like ALS**, also known as Lou Gehrig's disease) may have to face the possibility that once they are placed on the ventilator, they may not be able to get off of it again.[37] Your physician can help you assess whether or not the use of the ventilator is likely to be temporary or permanent.

**For those in respiratory failure, there are alternatives to the machine.** The physician may suggest using oxygen, a pressurized

---

\*   Chronic obstructive pulmonary disease
\*\*Amyotrophic lateral sclerosis

face mask, a special vest, or medications. As you can imagine, the fear of not being able to breathe can be just as great a burden as the shortness of breath itself. **Medications and supplemental oxygen can be used to address both the fear of being short of breath and the feeling of shortness of breath itself.**

I had a patient who had so much difficulty breathing when she moved from the chair to her bed, it took her a half hour to recover. Yet her chronic shortness of breath was treated very effectively with medication. This conservative elderly lady told me once, "I have always been opposed to drugs. But this morphine is wonderful because it allows me to breathe." Some patients find meditation, prayer, and guided imagery can also reduce anxiety, fear, and shortness of breath.

> *By removing the ventilator, we are allowing a natural death to occur that would have happened earlier if the machine had never been started.*

Sometimes patients are put on a ventilator with the hope that its use will be temporary until the pneumonia, heart failure, or other complication is cleared up. But then their health continues to decline with no hope for improvement. The patients or their decision makers may then consider withdrawing the machine, knowing death may occur. The physician can help to assess what the future might hold.

If the decision is made to remove the machine and tube, the patient will be kept comfortable. Pain medications, sedatives, and relaxants will be used as needed to make withdrawal of the artificial respiration more comfortable. The family may or may not want to be present. If religious ritual is important to the patient and family, they may want to have clergy present for a prayer before and after the removal of the ventilator.

When the ventilator is removed, the person may not die immediately. **Remember, if the patient does die after the withdrawal of** a machine, the death is from the disease that caused respiratory failure and NOT from turning off the machine. The patient is not being killed. By removing the ventilator, we are allowing a natural death to occur that would have happened earlier if the machine had never been started.[38]

## Treatment Option: Dialysis

Kidney (renal) failure can happen in one of two ways. People who have had kidney decline for a number of years can eventually move into what is known as end-stage renal disease (ESRD). Others may not have had problems before, but in a short time their kidneys fail in what is known as acute renal failure (ARF) or acute kidney injury. Both are very serious conditions, and some patients may be helped with dialysis.

Hemodialysis is the most common type of dialysis. During this treatment, blood is circulated from the body of the patient through a machine that "cleans" the blood of impurities, and pumps it back into the patient. Each treatment can take several hours and is usually required three times a week.

Most patients must travel to a dialysis center to receive these treatments. The dialysis process does not make many people feel better immediately; in fact, they often feel wiped out after each treatment. Patients may experience nausea, cramping, and symptoms of low blood pressure (sweating, dizziness, rapid heartbeat, and feeling faint) during the treatments. Many patients report a better quality of life on the days they are not dialyzed.

For frail, elderly patients with multiple medical problems, dialysis may not offer hope of living longer or better. For elderly patients on dialysis, 76% are hospitalized in the last year of life. Half of these patients are admitted to an intensive care unit (ICU).[39] One study found that 61% of elderly dialysis patients regretted ever starting the treatment.[40] Most nursing home residents either die or are in worse physical shape one year after starting the treatment. In one large, widely quoted study, not a single nursing home patient improved physical performance after a year of dialysis.[41]

An article in *The New York Times* states, "More conservative approaches to kidney disease do exist and can improve older patients' quality of life." The article goes on to quote Dr. Alvin H. Moss, a nephrologist at West Virginia University School of Medicine. "Medication to control blood pressure, treat anemia, and reduce swelling and pain, 'these are treatments that will keep people comfortable for long periods,'" Dr. Moss says. "'People [with advanced kidney disease who have not yet developed end-stage symptoms] choosing medical management could live 12 to 18 months, 23 months.' And spend less time in medical facilities."[42]

Patients on dialysis usually die from heart disease. **The second most common cause of death for end-stage renal disease, especially for patients over the age of 65, is a decision to stop dialysis and die from kidney failure.**[43] Patients with end-stage kidney disease who stop dialysis die, on average, seven days later.[44] Approximately one out of every four dialysis patients makes a decision to withdraw from dialysis before death.[45] These decisions are usually based on an assessment by patients that their quality of life is not satisfactory.

If the patient has one or more other serious medical problems, the risk of death is increased. These risk factors include older age, poor nutritional intake, and difficulty or inability to take care of oneself because of poor functional status.[46] The patient's physician and a kidney specialist (nephrologist) can help assess whether or not dialysis is likely to help a patient. Just like with tube feeding, a time-limited trial (see page 23) of dialysis may help the patient learn what the treatment is like and help everyone understand if there is any medical benefit.

If the decision is made to withhold or withdraw dialysis, palliative care, including hospice, is appropriate to ensure that the patient dies comfortably.

## Treatment Option: Antibiotics

Before the 1950s, most deaths were caused by infections like pneumonia. Antibiotics changed all that. Infections that were once killers often can now be cured. If a person can still swallow, then oral antibiotics pose only a few possible side effects. If an injection or IV is required, the side effects—which may include diarrhea, nausea, and vomiting—may prove to be minor when compared to the possible benefit of curing infection. Throughout most of our lives, antibiotics are routinely taken. But toward the end of life, one might consider not using these medications to allow a natural and peaceful death to occur.

The question of withholding antibiotics usually arises near the end of a long course of a disease like Alzheimer's.[36] Because of problems with swallowing and/or feeding tubes (see pages 20–22), patients with end-stage Alzheimer's are at higher risk of getting pneumonia. If pneumonia continues to recur after several courses of antibiotics, you may consider not trying them again. Although the medication might temporarily work, it does not cure the underlying problem of dementia, which continues to progress.

**Dying from pneumonia can be very peaceful.** It used to be called "the old person's friend" because of how gently it took someone who had long been disabled by disease. The doctor will help the patient and family sort through the pros and cons of withholding antibiotics. The physician can also find ways of assuring that the patient will be kept comfortable even though antibiotics are being withheld.

Although I used Alzheimer's as an illustration, not using antibiotics may be a course taken at the end of any disease. I have seen some cancer patients refuse their use. Sometimes the family members of permanently unconscious patients with pneumonia will continue the use of a feeding tube but withhold antibiotics and allow a natural death from the infection to occur.

## Treatment Option: Pacemakers and Implanted Defibrillators

"Growing old is no good," a 95-year-old nursing home resident with a pacemaker told me. I asked her when it got to being "no good." She thought for a moment and then said, "About 80." I asked, "What made it 'no good' then?" I had to know. Without hesitation she said, "When I couldn't do things for myself anymore."

I told her daughter of this conversation and she said, "Oh yeah, Mom used to be so independent. I remember the time I came into her home and found her standing on the kitchen table, changing light bulbs in the ceiling fixture." Talking to her further, it seemed as if she had mixed feelings about her mother's situation. "Did the pacemaker help her after it was implanted?" I asked. The daughter nodded, but added, "Still, I wish we had never put in the pacemaker."

Some people have electronic devices surgically implanted in their chest to help their heartbeats stay in a steady and relatively brisk rhythm (pacemakers), or to provide a shock to try to fix a potentially deadly heart rhythm (defibrillators). Pacemakers improve the quality of life for many people. Defibrillators save many lives. But as we have seen with ventilators and feeding tubes, the same medical interventions that can save lives may also become a burden too great to bear.

The daughter mentioned above felt as if a medical device that once improved her mother's quality of life later became a cause for suffering. In her view, shared by some medical experts, the pacemaker eventually became a barrier to a natural death and allowed her mother to live long enough to accumulate other medical problems. Had her mother died sooner, she would have been spared the additional suffering.

**As patients with a serious illness move toward the end of life, many choose to have these devices turned off.** The procedure to deactivate a device is quite simple. A healthcare professional can either reprogram the pacemaker or defibrillator by remote control or use a magnet. No surgery is needed, and the process is painless.

Death may or may not follow soon after the deactivation, depending on the nature and severity of the heart condition that the device was supposed to address in the first place. For those in the process of dying naturally, or those who are only being kept alive because of the pacemaker, deactivation can be followed by death within minutes. For others, death may take place within weeks or months. Sometimes, turning off a device has no immediate effect at all. A physician can let the patient and family know what to expect if a device is deactivated. Be assured that all patients who undergo deactivation can be kept comfortable and free from pain.

Implanted defibrillators create a special burden for patients who are dying. While a patient is otherwise healthy, this device attempts to reestablish healthy heart rhythms and can be life saving. But in the days, weeks, or months prior to death, repeated shocks in the chest can become a burden.

As the body is shutting down and organs are failing, the heart may enter unstable rhythms and will eventually stop naturally. In some cases, the defibrillator may sense the instability and hit the patient with painful electrical shocks.[47] Meanwhile, the patient's other medical conditions that are leading to death will continue to worsen.

According to medical ethics and the law, any life-prolonging or life-saving device that may be refused in the first place may be withdrawn at any time. Pacemakers and implanted defibrillators are no different in this sense than breathing machines, CPR, dialysis, or feeding tubes. A patient or their representative has the right to refuse any medical intervention or ask for its withdrawal.[48]

Turning off the device does not kill the patient. It is removing a barrier to natural death. If a patient dies soon after deactivation, then the cause of death is the underlying heart condition. **Deactivation is not killing the patient, nor assisting in a suicide,** but instead allowing a natural death. There may even be another condition—for example, cancer or pneumonia—which is the cause of death. In such cases, the deactivation had nothing to do with the cause or timing of a death.

A discussion about the possible deactivation of a device should be part of every patient's advance care planning. Physicians and other healthcare professionals will be able to advise patients about their particular situation, especially about when it is appropriate to turn off the implanted device.

## *Treatment Option: Pain Control*

Many serious illnesses have pain as a common problem. Fortunately, much can be done to reduce and eliminate any pain. Medications such as aspirin, acetaminophen (Tylenol), and morphine can be used to alleviate these troublesome symptoms. Other factors besides the disease itself can make pain worse. Depression, spiritual distress, broken family relationships, or lack of sleep can all contribute to increased pain.

Likewise, we know that many things besides drugs can alleviate pain. Some examples are: spiritual counsel from clergy, family, or friends; meditation; music; guided imagery; prayer; hypnosis; visits from family or friends; massage; and many others.

**Here are the facts regarding pain control:**[49]

- Doctors and/or nurses should ask patients regularly if they are experiencing pain. Never accept pain as inevitable. Always inform your healthcare providers if you are experiencing pain.

- It is important to take pain medications as prescribed. *The goal is to stay ahead of the pain,* not just to respond when the pain gets unbearable.

- Many patients remain clearheaded while taking pain medications. Others may feel drowsy. Drowsiness associated with some pain medications usually decreases after several days of taking the medicine.

- For patients with a serious, life-limiting, or terminal illness, the small risk of addiction is usually of little medical concern. For most of these patients, the benefit of strong pain medication outweighs the risk of addiction.[50] A clinician who specializes in palliative care can help assess this risk.

- Physicians usually increase doses of pain medications like morphine until they find the level needed to control pain. This gradual increase of the dose is called "titrating." Pain medication that is titrated slowly WILL NOT shorten the life of a patient, no matter how high the dosage gets.[51]

- Some patients may choose to be made unconscious by medications in the last hours or days of life if it is necessary to control pain or other symptoms. This is sometimes referred to as palliative sedation.[52]

# What to Do: Practical Help for Decision Making

Treatment decisions are made through an agreement among the physician, the competent patient, and the family. The medical team needs to know what the wishes of the patient are in regard to treatment decisions. This section covers things that can help you to arrive at a treatment plan and to see that the plan is implemented.

## Discuss the Issues

It is best for the patient, family, and doctors to have such a discussion before a crisis occurs that would require a decision in a time of stress. As with any treatment, you are entitled to a second opinion from another physician. If you have a difference of opinion with the attending physician, then you have a legal right to transfer the patient's care to another doctor. Likewise, a physician who feels he or she cannot ethically carry out the requests of a family or patient may withdraw from the case by arranging for another doctor to take over.

## Make an Intentional Decision

☐ **If you want all life-prolonging measures:** After you have discussed the treatment options and decided you would like to have life-prolonging measures applied, usually no special orders are required. These are standard procedures and will most likely be applied if there is no order restricting them. Delay in making a decision against life-prolonging measures may be interpreted to mean that you want all heroic measures used, including CPR and mechanical ventilators.

☐ **If you do not want CPR:** Ask the physician to write a DNR (do not resuscitate) order—also known as DNAR (do not attempt resuscitation), AND (allow natural death), No Code, or No CPR—on the medical record of the patient. If the patient is at home or in a residential care home, you may also ask the physician for an "out-of-hospital DNR" form that is honored by the rescue squad (see pages 11–12).

☐ **If you do not want a feeding tube inserted:** Discuss this with the physician. Generally, you have several days or weeks to make such a decision if a crisis does occur.

☐ **If you want artificial feeding withdrawn:** Also discuss this with the physician. You must prepare yourself, your family, and your friends emotionally to have such an order carried out. Any of these treatment decisions requires deep emotional involvement, but the decision to withdraw artificial feeding can be especially trying.

☐ **If you do not want to hospitalize someone living at home or residing in a long-term-care facility:** Consider contacting the attending physician about a "do not hospitalize" (DNH) order. Ask the doctor about options for keeping the patient comfortable and reaching the medical goals without a transfer to the hospital.

☐ **If you want to receive palliative care:** Again, this is an order the physician must write, so contact him or her about the order or for a referral to palliative care. Visit **www.getpalliativecare.org** for more information.

☐ **If you would like to receive a hospice care (comfort measures only) order:** A physician can write the order or refer you to hospice. You may also contact a local hospice directly or call The National Hospice and Palliative Care Organization (NHPCO) at 800-658-8898. Visit their website, **www.caringinfo.org.**

## Consider an Advance Directive

Advance directives generally come in two types: the living will and the Durable Power of Attorney for Healthcare (also know as a Healthcare Proxy or Lasting Power of Attorney). A person must be capable of making decisions in order to establish an advance directive. All states have some form of healthcare advance directive law, which provides for either a living will declaration, a healthcare proxy, or both.

- **Living will:** A competent person who does not want to have artificial life-prolonging procedures used when there is no hope of recovery might consider signing a living will. It is called a *living* will because the document takes effect while the person is still living. Typically, the declaration must be signed in the presence of witnesses who are not relatives. Someone holding a power of attorney or a guardian cannot sign the declaration on behalf of another person, but they most likely can make decisions for the patient.

  Usually this declaration states a person's wishes in the event that the person can no longer speak on his or her own behalf. Basically, the declaration says, "If I have a terminal condition, and there is no hope of recovery, I do not want my life prolonged by artificial means." You may add more specific language if you wish to declare that you *do* want your life artificially prolonged.

Although these laws and declarations are very helpful, some questions still remain. For example, "What is artificial?" As discussed in Chapter Two, some consider feeding tubes artificial and extraordinary, while others consider them natural and ordinary (see pages 16–17).

Also, "What is terminal?" In one sense, every human is terminal. If a person's heart stops, that is a terminal condition, but for a few patients the condition might be reversed by CPR. If a person cannot eat, that is a terminal condition, although it can be treated by artificial feeding.

In the end, the living will must be interpreted by the family and the physician. They must decide that indeed the ill person is in a "terminal condition, with no hope of recovery" and, therefore, no extraordinary measures will be used. Then they will choose which treatments are extraordinary.

Physicians are likely to want to know that *all* the family members agree with a decision to withhold or withdraw treatment, even if a living will has clearly stated the patient's desires. A living will is dependent on a family being unified in making sure the patient's wishes are honored. **The realities of the limitations of living wills emphasize how important it is to have open, honest family discussions about treatment choices.**

For more information about advance directives in the United States and to find a copy of one for your state, go to **www.caringinfo.org** or call 800-658-8898.

• **Durable Power of Attorney for Healthcare (also called a Healthcare Proxy):** This gives the person designated in the document authority to make any healthcare decision on behalf of patients who cannot make decisions for themselves. It covers all healthcare decisions, whether or not they relate to terminal illness. The job of the person designated to make decisions is to make choices the patient likely would have made. Many states now have standard forms to use, or you may want to contact a lawyer for advice regarding this document.

## Talk to Your Doctor about Physician Orders for Life Sustaining Treatment (POLST)

This form is available in many areas of the United States. The form is different from the two advance directives mentioned previously. The POLST form translates the values expressed in an advance directive into medical orders that are immediately active.

POLST aims to provide continuity of care for patients according to their preferences across all care settings (e.g., hospitals, hospice, long-term care, and home), and is transferred with the patient throughout the healthcare system (for example, from home or nursing home to the hospital). A doctor fills out the form after a discussion with the patient or family. A copy of the POLST form is included in the medical record while the original remains with the patient.

On the form, the physician writes orders based on the patient's preferences for treatments such as CPR, feeding tubes, hospitalization, and comfort care. Visit **www.polst.org** for more information.

## Questions to Help Make a Decision

- **What is the agreed-upon goal of medical care for the patient at this phase of life?** The three possible goals are cure, stabilization of functioning, or preparing for a comfortable and dignified death (see pages 3–4). Remember, the goals can be combined and will probably change over time, so this and all of these questions may need to be revisited from time to time.

- **What does the patient think about their current and probable future condition?** Patients with decision-making capacity can speak for themselves. If they are unable to express an opinion, then try to imagine what they would think about their current state. If the likely outcome of further life-prolonging procedures would be increased disability and/or greater mental decline, how would they feel about that? The purpose of this question is to consider what you think the patient values most.

- **What is in the best interest of the patient?** This is the question of *values*. This book has shown that there are differences of opinion regarding what is "best" for the patient. Some say it is best to keep a patient alive at all costs. Others say it is best to allow a patient to die and not prolong the dying process with artificial means.

- **What are the prognosis and probable consequences if a certain treatment plan is followed?** This is a question to discuss with a physician or an experienced nurse. Other related questions are:

  - What are the chances of survival after using CPR?

  - If the patient survives, what condition might the patient be in afterwards?

  - Does the physician anticipate just a temporary use of a feeding tube (or other machines) or might the patient live indefinitely, nonresponsive, in a debilitated state?

  - If we try a temporary use of the treatment and the patient does not improve significantly, can the treatment be discontinued?

  - Might death be expected, given the medical condition of the patient?

  - If death would be expected and acceptable, might we try not to cure any underlying condition, but prepare for a comfortable and dignified death?

- **Can I let go and just let things be?** This may be the most difficult question to answer. Occasionally, a family member will say, "I know my father would never want to be kept alive like this. I know it would be best if he just died. I know there is no hope of his recovery. But I can't let go." Most often, the view of what is medically, ethically, legally, or morally (according to one's own beliefs) appropriate treatment is totally influenced by the question, "Can I let go and let be?" This is discussed more thoroughly in the next chapter.

## Getting Help with End-of-Life Decisions

Are decisions regarding life-prolonging procedures black and white? No! There are often gray areas. As you gather more information, the answers will become clearer. Physicians, nurses, clergy, and social workers are just a few of the people who can help you sort out the decision. The medical staff caring for the patient will be as supportive as possible, no matter what the treatment decision.

### Chapter Four Summary:

- As a patient's condition declines, you may be faced with decisions about hospitalization, ventilator support, dialysis, or the use of antibiotics. For some patients these treatments are appropriate, and for others they may be withheld.

- Pacemakers and implanted defibrillators may hinder a peaceful death and can be deactivated.

- Written living wills and durable powers of attorney for health-care can be helpful, but the most important thing one can do for future care is to discuss your wishes with your family and physician.

- In making decisions about life-prolonging procedures, first establish the goal of medical care for the patient at this phase of life. Then learn about the probable consequences of continued treatment or withdrawal, and consider what the patient wants and what's in his or her best interest.

- If most of the signs seem to be pointing toward withholding or withdrawing treatment, the big question is, "Can I let go and let be?"

# Chapter Five:

## The Journey to Letting Be—
## The Emotional and Spiritual Issues

**This chapter will answer the following questions:**
- What are the author's personal opinions about each of the treatment options?
- Is it possible to let go and let be?
- Are there others who have experienced "letting go and letting be" who can show us the way?

Since 1983, I have served as a chaplain in a nursing home, a hospice, and a hospital at various times. My convictions on life-prolonging procedures have grown out of my pastoral relationship with patients and their families. My teachers have been the patients and their families, caring nurses and physicians, medical research, and writings reflecting on the emotional and spiritual struggles at the end of life.

### A Personal Word from a Chaplain

Here is where I am today on each of the four most common treatment decisions for patients toward the end of their lives. **Although I believe my opinions have a solid foundation in research and my own professional experience, nothing can substitute for a discussion of these issues with your physician, family, and spiritual advisors.**

### My Opinion on CPR

I recognize that 17% of hospital patients do survive after cardio-pulmonary resuscitation (CPR). A physician can help the patient and the family assess if resuscitation attempts offer any possible medical benefit. However, the evidence overwhelmingly shows that CPR is not able to restore most patients who are at the end of a serious illness to their previous level of functioning. CPR is of no medical benefit to these patients.

In two studies, almost all of the nursing home patients who were successfully resuscitated and discharged from the hospital refused any further CPR attempts.[53,54] I think this speaks about their own or their family's assessment of the benefits and burdens of CPR.

I believe the practice of discussing CPR with patients at the end of their lives or their families is a cruel hoax. The hoax is that we approach those making medical decisions for the patient and ask whether or not to use CPR, which implies that it offers some benefit. The most cruel part is this may seem like asking, "Do you want us to attempt CPR or do you want us to let your mother die?" Who wants their mother to die?

*Refusing resuscitation attempts is not giving up hope on life.*

The fact is, that is the wrong question. These patients are going to die with or without CPR. For various reasons (some of them very good), healthcare practices do NOT require us to ask permission to do a treatment (CPR) that has been proven not only to be ineffective but even harmful to certain patients. Therefore, we make patients and families feel as if they are making the choice to let someone die. The real choice is whether the patient will die a more peaceful death or spend his or her final moments attempting to reverse certain death with all the force of aggressive medical care.

**My observation has been that families who want their dying relatives to receive CPR are actually having a difficult time letting go and letting be.** They have watched the slow decline of a once vital person. For them to say "do not use CPR" feels like saying "I give up hope."

Refusing resuscitation attempts is not giving up hope on life. It is facing the fact that there is no hope that CPR will save the life of this patient. CPR becomes merely a symbol of how the healthcare team and caregivers never gave up trying. But since it offers no medical benefit, it is a meaningless symbol. A genuine question a family must ask is, "Do we want Mother to receive CPR for *us* or for *her?* Is it because we cannot accept the fact that she is going to die some day that we want everything done to keep her alive?" **Often the most loving thing to do is to let loved ones die in peace without the aggressiveness of CPR.**

## *My Opinion on Artificial Nutrition and Hydration*

I have seen many patients benefit from the use of a feeding tube. One of the best friends I made at the nursing home was a 42-year-old Navy Commander who had ALS (Lou Gehrig's disease). Sometimes he could talk with difficulty, but when he couldn't talk, he would use his toe to draw letters in order to spell out words. We would discuss world events, tell jokes, and share stories about our families.

His life was sustained by a mechanical respirator and by a feeding tube. He found a way to make the best of his situation. Given the same handicaps, I hope I would choose to go on with life as he did. Fortunately, he was competent and could make his own choice to be kept alive through artificial means.

I have been involved in more than a dozen cases where artificial feeding was begun and later stopped, allowing the person to die. One case involved an 83-year-old woman who suffered a stroke and had a feeding tube inserted. She never again made any significant response to her environment. Two and a half years after the stroke, her leg broke when the nurses were routinely turning her. Her three sons were convinced she would never have wanted to be sustained like that, and they asked the doctor to withdraw the artificial feeding and let her die.

A 40-year-old woman had a brain tumor and, through a series of events, ended up in a persistent vegetative state after undergoing an operation. She received feeding through a tube for more than two years. The patient's physician told the family, "If this were my daughter, I would stop the feedings and let her die." The family agreed and took her home to spend her last days.

Years after the patient's death, I was visiting with her mother. She said, "You helped me so much as we were struggling with our decision. Remember the day I came into your office crying, worried that I would be killing my daughter if we stopped the feedings?" I told her I remembered it well. She went on, "You told me I wasn't killing her, but the brain tumor was."

Another woman had been at the nursing home for about five years and had survived two strokes. She was able to sit in a wheelchair, eat, and visit with her family, but she was not satisfied with her quality of life. She had a third stroke, which the family had expected. Rather than rush her to the hospital, where she would likely have received a feeding tube against her wishes, the family and physician decided to keep her at the nursing home.

She could not take in any food or fluid by mouth. She was alert, and her eyes seemed to follow people as they moved around the room. We kept her comfortable and free from pain. She died peacefully a week later. This family made the courageous decision not to start a feeding tube that would only prolong the dying process, perhaps for years.

Ideally, people should make an intentional choice either to accept or refuse artificial feedings. My observations have led me to believe that often people will receive feeding tubes as a default, without the doctors allowing families or patients to make a choice. I am sure physicians are afraid of the legal ramifications of "not trying everything."

I wish physicians would offer a time-limited trial of a feeding tube (see page 23). If the feeding tube does not have the desired effect in the specified time, then a choice could be made to continue or discontinue it. But people get into a situation where they had hoped a tube would be temporary, and years later the patient has still not made any sort of response.

Some families do make a conscious choice to continue tube feedings even when there is no response from the patient. The daughter of one such patient told me, "I could never not feed Mother." I respected her position. If she decided to withdraw the tube, she—not I—would have to live with that decision. I know she was sure she would feel guilty if she approved of the withdrawal of treatment and let her mother die. In the whole of human history, it is only in this generation that families feel guilty if they do not artificially feed someone who stops eating at the end of life.

Many other cultures see stopping eating as a sign of dying and not its cause.[55] They never even consider the use of a feeding tube. We humans stop taking in food and fluid as our systems naturally shut down. It was like we were created to go out of this world as gently as possible, and the way we have done this since the beginning of time is to stop eating and drinking at the end of life. Yet, now, some would say we are "starving a patient to death" if we do not artificially force feed them.

*Many other cultures see stopping eating as a sign of dying and not its cause. They never even consider the use of a feeding tube.*

Like the patients in a permanently unconscious state, I believe that artificial feeding of those with end-stage Alzheimer's disease or other types of dementia is a totally inappropriate treatment. It does not cure the underlying disease, it does not prevent death, and it does not even offer a longer life than for those who do not receive a tube. The numerous burdens of a feeding tube for these patients are not counterbalanced by any benefits (see pages 20–22).

This opinion gets personal for me. I have very strong feelings about how inappropriate it is to put a feeding tube in end-stage dementia patients. I base my opinion on the medical research and my family's experience. My grandmothers and almost all of my 13 aunts and uncles lived with dementia.

One of my aunts had a feeding tube. After my father watched his sister languish for years with the feeding tube, he knew he did not want one. Both of my parents suffered from dementia and both stopped eating in their last days. Their clear wishes were never to have a feeding tube. My sister, brother, and I honored those wishes. Both parents had the most peaceful deaths within two weeks of when they stopped eating.

As in the case of CPR, treatment with feeding tubes has become symbolic. All cultures through all ages offer food and water as a sign of hospitality and caring. But when a patient can no longer receive sustenance by mouth, artificially supplied feeding no longer carries the same meaning for me.

Artificially fed patients receive little of the emotional and spiritual support a patient may receive through hand feeding, although they obviously can be loved and cared for in other ways. But artificial feeding for terminally ill, dying, or otherwise failing patients becomes only a symbol for the family and has little medical benefit for the patient.

*Artificial feeding for terminally ill, dying, or otherwise failing patients becomes only a symbol for the family and has little medical benefit for the patient.*

I have seen a more powerful symbol of caring than using a feeding tube. In my early years as a nursing home chaplain, a woman came to us from the hospital with a feeding tube that she had received after a stroke. After she repeatedly pulled it out, a nurse, her daughter, and I went in to

> *"The ultimate tragedy is…dying in an alien and sterile arena, separated from the spiritual nourishment that comes from being able to reach out to a loving hand."*
>
> —Norman Cousins

speak with the patient. The patient clearly understood she would die without the tube, and that was her wish. The daughter accepted her mother's decision.

I will never forget the last time I saw them. I rounded the corner to enter the patient's room, only to see that her daughter had climbed into bed with her mother. The younger woman cradled her elderly mother gently in her arms. They were silent. Words were not required. Which is a more powerful symbol of love and caring? A daughter cuddling her mother in her last days or artificially supplied feeding? If I were dying, I would wish for the loving touch.

I am reminded of the words of Norman Cousins: "Death…is not the ultimate tragedy. The ultimate tragedy is depersonalization…, dying in an alien and sterile arena, separated from the spiritual nourishment that comes from being able to reach out to a loving hand."[56]

## *My Opinion on Hospitalization*

By design, hospitals are more aggressive in the treatment of diseases. When patients are in declining health and have an acute illness, it is often appropriate to provide care only in the nursing home, assisted living, memory care, or at home. I have seen this done very effectively.

Sometimes hospitalization seems to be the only choice for an injury like a hip fracture. However, I have known a number of families (including my own) who refused hospitalization for a hip fracture and kept the patient comfortable where they were. On the other hand, I have been amazed at the recovery of some very elderly patients from a hip replacement. Still, hospitalization for such surgery is sometimes the beginning of the end.

I have no real sense of how to know ahead of time into which category a patient might fall. **We do know that 50% of all end-stage dementia patients who are hospitalized for a hip fracture or pneumonia will die within six months,** as compared to 12–13% of mentally intact patients.[57] Families and patients must confer with physicians and nurses as to what is appropriate for this patient at this time. As a general rule, hospitalization should be reserved for patients who cannot have their comfort needs or treatment goals met at the place where they reside, but might have these needs met in the hospital.

### My Opinion on Hospice and the Comfort Measures Only Order

Hospice is most effective when a patient and family enter a program months before the patient actually dies. An earlier shift to a comfort measures only order for nursing home, assisted living, or home-bound patients is also ideal.

Sadly, some people put off shifting the focus from attempts to cure to improving quality of life until the very end stage of the disease process. These patients and families miss the full benefit of hospice and the comfort measures only order.

The beauty of this approach is that the family, patient, and medical team are no longer being consumed with aggressive attempts to achieve a cure. All physical symptoms continue to be addressed, but the emphasis shifts to the alleviation of pain and to giving emotional and spiritual care to the dying person and the family.

With cure no longer being the primary goal, the patient and family are able to do the difficult—but more important—work of improving the patient's quality of life, saying goodbye, grieving together, and sharing in one of the most important events in the life of the family.

# Taking the First Steps in the Journey to Letting Be

## Changing the Treatment Plan

One of my goals in writing this book was to introduce those who are making medical care decisions for a patient to the wide range of what is acceptable from legal, ethical, moral, and medical points of view. What makes the difference in choosing one treatment plan over another?

In my years of experience as a healthcare chaplain, I have thought much about medical interventions on behalf of patients at the end of their lives. I have considered CPR, artificial feeding, IV therapy, hospitalization, and even the use of antibiotics and diagnostic tests on dying patients. Often, in the eyes of my colleagues on the medical team and in my own opinion, these treatments are not medically indicated, are marginal in their benefit (if there is any benefit at all), increase the burden of living, possibly prolong the dying process, and are not required by ethics, medicine, law, morality, or faith. Why are they done?

Perhaps the reason these treatments are pursued is that the family has not been able to let go (and the physician has also not been able to let go or has not informed the decision makers of the marginal benefit of such treatment plans). **Those who choose such life-prolonging treatments for failing patients do so primarily out of an inability to let go and not out of moral necessity or medical appropriateness.**[58,59] How else can you explain such a wide range of treatment choices for similarly afflicted patients?

I often see these emotional and spiritual struggles overwhelming all other considerations. Caregivers who share cultural and religious backgrounds will still choose different treatment plans because one caregiver is having a harder time letting go. This is especially obvious when brothers and sisters choose different treatments for an ailing parent. I have many times heard, "The rest of us had made the decision to let Mom go, but our brother wasn't ready yet."

Another reason I know that decisions are mostly based on the emotional and spiritual struggle of letting go is because I have seen so many family members change from an aggressive treatment plan to withdrawal of curative treatment. Decision makers do not usually have a change of mind about ethics, law, morality, or religion. They have a change of heart. They finally come to the point of being able to let go and just let things be.

## Words to Try When Talking with a Sick Person

| When you want to say: | Try this instead: |
| --- | --- |
| Dad, you are going to be just fine. | Dad, are there some things you worry about? |
| Don't talk like that! You can beat this! | It must be hard to come to terms with all of this. |
| I can't see how anyone can help. | We will be there for you, always. |
| I just can't talk about this. | I am feeling a little overwhelmed right now. Can we take this up later tonight? |
| What do the doctors know? You might live forever. | Do you think the doctors are right? How does it seem to you? |
| Please don't give up. I need you here. | I need you here. I will miss you terribly. But we will get through somehow. |
| There has to be something more to do. | Let's be sure we get the best of medical treatments, but let's be together when we have done all we can. |
| Don't be glum. You will get well. | It must be hard. Can I just sit with you for a while? |

From *Handbook for Mortals: Guidance for People Facing Serious Illness,* 2nd Edition, page 11, by Joanne Lynn, Joan Harrold, and Janice Schuster, Copyright © 2011 by Oxford University Press. Used by permission.

## The Emotional Nature of the Struggle:
## Treating the Wrong Person

A friend came to me on a Monday and was fighting back tears when she said, "I have to make a life-and-death decision about my mother by Thursday." My friend was about a three-hour drive from the town where her mother was hospitalized. Her 82-year-old mother's health had been failing for two years.

In that time she had two strokes, was in kidney failure, and now was in the hospital on dialysis. My friend and her family were facing the decision of whether or not to withdraw the dialysis. Thinking of the questions to help make a decision (see pages 51–53), I asked, "How effectively is the dialysis working?"

My friend said, "Oh. The doctors say it isn't doing any good."

I asked, "Did your mother ever give any indication of what she would have wanted?"

"Yes. She said she never wanted to be on dialysis," she replied.

I couldn't believe what I was hearing. I said, "I am going to be straight with you. This is not a hard decision. There is no question that you should stop treatment. What is going on here that makes this so difficult?"

She began to choke up again, fighting back tears. "I guess I feel guilty for not having visited my mother enough these last couple of years," she said. At least she was honest enough with herself to know the real issue: A patient was being treated miles away in order to take care of a daughter's guilt. This happens more often than we would like to admit.

In another situation, a physician wrote an order to start an IV to hydrate a dying patient, and he said to the nurse, "We're doing this for the family." He knew that this treatment probably would not add to the patient's comfort and might even contribute to her discomfort. But he was doing something for an emotionally distraught family.

I wish he had said to the family, "I know you are struggling with the fact that your mother is dying. None of us wants to lose our mother. But starting an IV will not help her, nor stop her eventual death. I am concerned about you and want the nurse to call the chaplain or social worker so you can talk about your struggles. We will keep your mother comfortable and as free from pain as possible."

Sometimes it seems easier to aggressively treat patients, perhaps even for years, than to help families confront the emotional and spiritual issues that are driving the treatment choices. Indeed, physicians are trained to order medical treatments and not necessarily to help patients and families with the more difficult struggles in their souls. It is understandable that doctors would try to address a family's emotional struggle by ordering aggressive treatment of the patient. The problem is, they are treating the wrong person.

## Can I Let Go and Let Be?

Once a patient's daughter told me, as her father was very close to death, "I know a 'no CPR' order is the best thing, but I just can't let go." She wasn't talking about medical or even ethical decisions. She was in the midst of an emotional struggle to let go. Her holding on was just an illusion. Perhaps she felt CPR attempts would allow her to hold on to her father for just a little longer, but that treatment could not accomplish that goal. She finally requested the "no CPR" order only days before his death.

We had another patient in his 80s fed by an artificial feeding tube. In four years at the nursing home, he rarely made any response to those around him. His wife could answer the questions I asked to help her make a decision whether or not to withdraw the artificial feeding and let her husband die. She said, "I know he would never have wanted to be kept alive like this. I know it would be best if he just died. I know he will never get better. But I just can't let go."

She struggled with the withdrawal of treatment decision for more than two years. It finally came down to a meeting with an administrator, a daughter, the wife, her pastor, and me. We reviewed the patient's condition and what his wishes would have been. The minister asked if the administrator and I would leave the room for a minute.

When he called us back in, the wife said she had decided to withdraw the treatment and let her husband die. She signed a document authorizing the withdrawal of artificial feeding. I will never forget her next words: "I feel like a great burden has been lifted from my shoulders." She was able to let go and let be.

Can you let go and let be? Of course you can, though some people never do. And it can take a long or a short time. As a pastoral caregiver, I wonder how I can help families and patients come to the place of letting go and letting be.

I even called three family members of two patients who had died years before following the withdrawal of artificial feeding. I asked each, "Did you have any regrets in your decision to withdraw treatment?" Without knowing what the others had said, they each immediately responded, "Yes, and I regret that we did not withdraw treatment sooner." Then I asked, "Was there anything either I or the nursing center could have done to help you come to this decision sooner?" Again, they all responded, "No. It just takes time."

It is because of this element of time that I have seen the families of dementia patients tend to more readily accept letting go of the patient in the end. Because of the slow progression of diseases like Alzheimer's, the family has had to let go of parts of this person for years. They have already been grieving and letting go, and therefore they find saying "no CPR" or "no artificial feeding" is the next step in releasing this person.

I do not mean to imply that this decision is easy for anyone. Yet, because of the emotional nature of these decisions, families of patients with dementia have already begun the process of letting go and letting be.

## A Lifetime of Letting Go

After describing the difficult and sometimes painful struggles people endure when letting go of someone at the end of life, a massage therapist friend of mine said, "This is the same issue my clients are dealing with. They come with a stiff neck or back pain. They have to learn how to let go." I thought it was a fitting parallel.

**A natural response to the possibility of losing someone is to hold on tighter or to try to gain more control. But this does not lead to a life of freedom and joy, the very things we were pursuing.**

Most of us do learn to let go. We let go of our childhood and accept adult responsibilities. We let go of our teenage children and our attempts to control them. We let go of finding happiness in possessions or careers. We even learn that we have to let go of other people and not be dependent on them for our happiness. To learn these lessons, we have to accept the fact that these things or people were gifts in the first place.

*Because of the emotional nature of these decisions, families of patients with dementia have already begun the process of letting go and letting be.*

There are two ways to hold on. We can grasp tightly as we would a coin in our fist. We fear we will lose it, so we hold it tight. Indeed, if we open our hand palm down, the coin falls from our possession, and we feel cheated. The other way to hold on is by opening our hand palm up. The coin may sit there, or it could be blown away or shaken out of our possession. But while it is there, we are privileged to have it. We hold on with an open hand. Our hand is relaxed and we experience freedom.[60]

I do not want to oversimplify the deep struggles within our hearts as we make end-of-life decisions. **Yet I am convinced that letting go and letting be is a way of life that can be experienced**

**throughout our lifetime.** Grasping, controlling individuals tend to be so to the very end of life. Those who live life with a sense of gift and grace also tend to do so to the very end of life.[61] Daniel Callahan writes,

> "How we die will be an expression of how we have wanted to live, and the meaning we find in our dying is likely to be at one with the meaning we have found in our living.... [A] person who has learned how to let life go may have not only a richer and more flexible life, but also one that better prepares him for his decline."[62]

Throughout most of our lives, aggressive curative medical treatment is appropriate. Those who live life with a sense of grace and letting go can seek a cure from diseases from which they would have a reasonable opportunity to recover. But those who have a sense of giftedness of life have an easier time letting go when treatment has a limited potential of cure and a greater possibility of increasing burden.

*When I can no longer have this gift of life, I do not have to grasp it either for myself or for those I love.*

Two studies uncovered the fact that CPR is used less in religious nursing homes.[9,63] It was not the purpose of these studies to find out why there is less CPR in these religious facilities, but one reason may be because they have a positive view of life after death. I do not feel that adequately explains the difference in the use of CPR.

My guess is that the administration and staff have a sense that life is a gift and to hold on too tightly is to betray the sense of giftedness. They live daily with an open hand, appreciating each moment and not having to control events—including not having to stop death. By their presence, they then communicate this lifestyle to patients and families. I hope my faith is a faith for living fully each day with a sense of grace and gift. Then when I can no longer have this gift of life, I do not have to grasp it either for myself or for those I love.

## Some Religious Questions

Sometimes a family member, when choosing aggressive life-prolonging treatment like CPR or a mechanical ventilator, says something like, "When God calls a person home, then they will go, no matter what we do." The patient then continues to be kept alive on the machine. But I believe that some things we do can stop people from being "called home."

**What greater message could a body be giving us that it is "time to go" than the heart stopping?** When a body can no longer take in food in the natural way, we might be "playing God" by inserting a feeding tube. Then again, we might be playing God by not using all the technology "He has given us." There are no easy answers.

I would rather not make assumptions about what God is trying to tell us through someone's medical condition. Not that we should approach these decisions without prayer and the guidance of our spiritual counselors, but we cannot presume that God is trying to tell us something one way or the other. Just because we have been "blessed" with certain technology does not mean we are obligated to use it.

On my first visit into the home of a woman with advanced metastatic cancer, the husband said, "Hank, God has told me that my wife is not going to die. So I don't want any negative talk about death and dying, only positive thoughts of healing." I said I would honor that, adding that I usually let the patient and family set the agenda. So if someone else in the family wanted to talk about the topic of dying, I would discuss it.

A month or so later, they had gotten the news that the cancer had spread to yet another organ. When I arrived for a visit, the husband was preparing to leave for work. "You know how I told you that God has told me my wife is going to live?" he started.

"Well, I still believe that, but Satan is trying to get me to doubt it. Would you pray for me?" I said of course I would. He left and I turned to his wife and asked her if she had as much confidence that she would not die as her husband did. She said no and began to cry. Through her tears she said, "I am afraid if I die I will be disappointing my husband."

On my next visit I told him what she had said. He sat close to her, took her hand, and assured her that she could never disappoint him. I said I had two concerns about only talking of healing in the midst of such a grave condition. "My first is that you may not adequately control the pain under the logic that, since you believe she is not dying, she only needs Tylenol." I continued, "My other concern is that you will miss having some very important conversations if you do not allow for the possibility of death. We all need to live as if each day were our last, but in your situation, having that attitude is most important."

After her death he said that he knew that God told him she would not die because God felt he wouldn't be able to handle the truth. I don't like to speak for God, but I just do not believe that the Lord would intentionally tell us lies. In my opinion, this man wanted so badly to hear the words "your wife will not die" that he imagined it came from God.

It was perfectly understandable for him not to want to lose his wife. And it was surely appropriate to pray for healing. But I believe we are on dangerous ground thinking we get a clear divine message that someone with advanced end-stage cancer will not die when the death expectancy rate for *all* of us is 100%.

## The Spiritual Nature of the Struggle

Although a few may have these questions about God or religion, we all ask the deeper spiritual questions as we contemplate the end of life. When I say "spiritual," try not to think of religion, a place of worship, or an organized way of thinking about God.

I am using the word in the broader sense of "that which gives life ultimate meaning."

Spiritual, in this sense, denotes that essence of ourselves that is greater than the flesh and bones that we inhabit. We are confronted most profoundly with our spiritual nature when someone we love is dying or does die. After the breath of life has gone out and the blood no longer gives vitality to the flesh, what is the meaning of this person's life?

**Sadly, most people spend much of their life avoiding this ultimate question.**[64-66] We surround ourselves with things and activities to mask the reality of the truth of our impermanence. We grasp on to life and our loved ones who are on the edge of dying. But the grasping can bring as much spiritual pain as the dying process itself. Many times I sat in our hospice team meeting as we discussed a family who was struggling so hard to hold on. They were grasping and controlling. I have said, "Dying is hard enough as it is. These people are making it so much harder than it needs to be."

Sogyal Rinpoche writes, "We are terrified of letting go, terrified, in fact, of living at all, since learning to live is learning to let go. And this is the tragedy and the irony of our struggle to hold on: not only is it impossible, but it brings us the very pain we are seeking to avoid."[68]

This teaching of the impermanence of life can be found in all cultures, religions, and ages. The Psalmist wrote, "For He knows how we were made; He remembers that we are dust. As for mortals, their days are like grass; they flourish like a flower of the field; for the wind passes over it, and it is gone, and its place knows it no more."[69]

> *"God, grant me the serenity to accept the things I cannot change, the courage to change the things I can, and the wisdom to know the difference."*[67]
>
> —*Reinhold Niebuhr*

Yet it seems in our current culture, we make every effort to deny its existence and fight to the very end, to "say it ain't so." **It is at this point—whether or not we accept the certainty of our own death and the deaths of those we love—where making end-of-life decisions becomes, at its core, a spiritual issue.** To let go, we must have the sense that this person will be okay, even in death.

## Giving Up, Letting Go, and Letting Be

A psychotherapist told me that a man who was struggling with AIDS once said, "I have finally learned the difference between giving up and letting go." I reflect often on his thoughts and see them as a struggle we all go through. This is especially true as we wrestle with end-of-life decisions.

> **"Giving Up, Letting Go, and Letting Be," by Hank Dunn**
>
> Giving up implies a struggle
>   Letting go implies a partnership
>     Letting be implies, in reality, there is nothing that separates
>
> Giving up says there is something to lose
>   Letting go says there is something to gain
>     Letting be says it doesn't matter
>
> Giving up dreads the future
>   Letting go looks forward to the future
>     Letting be accepts the present as the only moment I ever have
>
> Giving up lives out of fear
>   Letting go lives out of grace and trust
>     Letting be just lives
>
> Giving up is defeat at the hands of suffering
>   Letting go is victory over suffering
>     Letting be knows suffering is often in my own mind in the first place
>
> Giving up is unwillingly yielding control to forces beyond myself
>   Letting go is choosing to yield to forces beyond myself
>     Letting be acknowledges that control and choices can be illusions
>
> Giving up believes that God is to be feared
>   Letting go trusts in God to care for me
>     Letting be never asks the question

The truth is that we will die whether we give up, let go, or let be. We are making a choice about the nature of our dying or the dying of one we love. We can choose to die in trust and grace or in fear and struggle.

Perhaps I titled my book improperly. We are not faced with many hard choices. We are faced with one hard choice: **Can we let go and live life out of grace or must we hold on out of fear? Can we just let things be?** That is really what we are talking about. To withhold or withdraw artificial and mechanical devices is just returning the patient to a natural state. We are accepting what is. We have come to accept that the patient is dying and we will just let be.[70]

*We are making a choice about the nature of our dying—we can choose to die in trust and grace or in fear and struggle.*

Viktor Frankl was a psychiatrist and a Jew who was imprisoned for several years in Nazi concentration camps. As he observed the behavior of the inmates, of the guards, and of himself, he asked the question, "Can life have meaning in such horrible conditions?" His answer was "yes."

I refer to those who suffered under the Nazis not to downplay their suffering. Indeed, their suffering was horrifying and at the hands of an evil that none of us hope to ever have to face. That is my point. If these victims, in such dreadful circumstances, can find hope and meaning, surely I can in whatever hardships life brings my way.

Of the many stories Frankl relates, I have been most moved by the reflections of a young woman in a concentration camp as she lay dying. In this story is the essence of letting go and letting be and the assurance that the universe is essentially a caring place:

> This young woman knew that she would die in the next few days. But when I talked to her she was cheer-

ful in spite of this knowledge. "I am grateful that fate has hit me so hard," she told me. "In my former life I was spoiled and did not take spiritual accomplishments seriously."

Pointing through the window of the hut, she said, "This tree here is the only friend I have in my loneliness." Through that window she could see just one branch of a chestnut tree, and on the branch were two blossoms. "I often talk to this tree," she said to me. I was startled and didn't quite know how to take her words. Was she delirious? Did she have occasional hallucinations? Anxiously I asked her if the tree replied. "Yes." What did it say to her? She answered, "It said to me, 'I am here—I am here—I am life, eternal life.'"[71]

If a woman dying in a concentration camp can see that there is goodness and that there is life, then what is wrong with my vision if I cannot see the same?

## Fatal Isn't the Worst Outcome

Often we gain the greatest insights on how to live from those closest to death or those living with a serious illness. Flannery O'Connor was a well-known writer. For the last 13 years of her life she lived with lupus, a crippling and often painful disease. Her father died of the same illness when she was a teenager. She was just 39 at her death. I'm sure she would rather have lived longer and not been so disabled. But she was a person of deep faith and learned the lessons life sent her way. She wrote:

> "I have never been anywhere but sick. In a sense, sickness is a place, more instructive than a long trip to Europe, and it's always a place where there's no company; where nobody can follow. Sickness before death is a very appropriate thing and I think those who don't have it miss one of God's mercies."[72]

Many who have a near-death experience in which they were considered dead and are brought back to life report that the "other side" is a wonderful place and their fear of death is gone.[73-75] Their lives are changed for the better after that experience.

Sandol Stoddard reports conversations with hospice patients:

> "Let me tell you, Doctor," said an 83-year-old Hospice of Marin patient, "dying is the experience of a lifetime." What she meant by these splendid words remains, like the fabric of life itself, a mystery.

> "I think I was meant to come here," says Lillian Preston's final letter from St. Christopher's Hospice, "so that at last, I could experience joy."

> "I never knew how to live until I came here to die," said an elderly, blind gentleman of St. Joseph's Hospice in London.[76]

Certainly families, friends and the larger community are saddened and grieve the loss of a loved one. Yet we still have to incorporate this loss into our larger understanding of the meaning of life. Etty Hillesum, who would eventually die in the Auschwitz concentration camp, wrote about her contemplation of her own death. She said,

> "The reality of death has become a definite part of my life; my life has, so to speak, been extended by death, by my looking death in the eye and accepting it, by accepting destruction as part of life and no longer wasting my energies on fear of death or the refusal to acknowledge its inevitability. **It sounds paradoxical: by excluding death from our life we cannot live a full life, and by admitting death into our life we enlarge and enrich it.**"[77]

My wish is that patients with serious and life-threatening illnesses, their families, and physicians would have the grace to accept that a time comes when certain medical treatments only prolong the dying process. May they also have the wisdom to know when that time comes. And in those moments of letting go and letting be, may they have a sense of being upheld by a loving God in the midst of a caring universe.

Philosophers, sages, and saints through the ages often show a profound appreciation that **the essence of life is to live each day fully and that a life is not negated by death.** My hope is that patients and families will concentrate on living each day fully while accepting modern medicine's inability to extend the length of life indefinitely.

As conservationist Edward Abbey mused about the ending of his short 62 years, he commented, "It is not death or dying which is tragic, but rather to have existed without fully participating in life is the deepest personal tragedy."[78] Dr. Bernie Siegel works with people who are living with cancer. He has formed groups for patients called ECaP groups, for Exceptional Cancer Patients. A group member said one day, "Fatal isn't the worst outcome." And Siegel adds, "Not living is the worst outcome."[79]

My message to those who are taking this journey to letting go and letting be is one of hope. **We can live each day fully, even as we accept the certainty of our own death and that of those we love. To accept medicine's inability to put off death indefinitely is not a defeat.** It is accepting the world as it was created, while at the same time having a profound sense that the Creator has granted life as a gift. For me to hold on and grasp out of fear is to deny the gift and the Giver. Having walked this journey to letting be with hundreds of patients and families, I only have a greater sense of the wonderfulness of life.

Hank Dunn

Chaplain

# Endnotes

For a full listing of the endnotes and additional references, go to **www. hankdunn.com/references.**

### Introduction

1. Lynn J. Dying and dementia (editorial). *JAMA.* 1986;256:2244–5.
2. Kaldjian LC, Curtis AE, Shinkunas LSA, Cannon KT. Goals of care toward the end of life: A structured literature review. *Am J Hosp Palliat Care.* 2009;25(6):501–11.

### Chapter One: CPR—Cardiopulmonary Resuscitation

3. Rea TD, Fahrenbruch C, Culley L, et al. CPR with Chest Compression Alone or with Rescue Breathing. *N Engl J Med.* 2010;363:423–33.
4. Standards and Guidelines for Cardiopulmonary Resuscitation (CPR) and Emergency Cardiac Care (ECC). *JAMA.*1986;255(21):2905–2984.
5. Girotra S, Nallamothu BK, Spertus JA, et al. Trends in survival after in-hospital cardiac arrest. *N Engl J Med.* 2012;367:1912–20.
6. Sehatzadeh S. Cardiopulmonary resuscitation in patients with terminal illness: An evidence-based analysis. *Ont Health Technol Assess Ser.* 2014;14(15):1–38.
7. Applebaum GE, King JE, Finucane TE. The outcome of CPR initiated in nursing homes. *J Am Geriatr Soc.* 1990;38(3):197–200.
8. Booth CM, Boone RH, Tomlinson G, Detsky AS. Is this patient dead, vegetative, or severely neurologically impaired? Assessing outcome for comatose survivors of cardiac arrest. *JAMA.* 2004;291(7):870–9.
9. Duthie E, Mark D, Tresch D, Kartes S, Neahring J, Aufderheide T. Utilization of CPR in nursing homes in one community: Rates and nursing home characteristics. *J Am Geriatr Soc.* 1993;41(4):384–8.

### Chapter Two: Feeding Tubes—Artificial Nutrition and Hydration

10. Cranford RE. The persistent vegetative state: The medical reality (getting the facts straight). *Hastings Center Report.* 1988;18(1):27–32.
11. Peck A, Cohen CE, Mulvihill MN. Long-term enteral feeding of aged demented nursing home patients. *J Am Geriatr Soc.* 1990;38(11):1195–8.
12. Zopf Y, Konturek P, Nuernberger A, et al. Local infection after placement of percutaneous endoscopic gastrostomy tubes: A prospective study evaluating risk factors. *Can J Gastroenterol.* 2008;22(12):987–991.
13. Teno JM, Gozalo P, Mitchell SL, Kuo S, Fulton AT, Mor V. Feeding tubes and the prevention or healing of pressure ulcers. *Arch Intern Med.* 2012;172(9):697–701.
14. Hoefler JM. Making decisions about tube feeding for severely demented patients at the end of life: clinical, legal, and ethical considerations. *Death Stud.* 2000;24(3):233–54.
15. Curtis E. Harris, who is both a physician and a lawyer, states "I do not consider the provision of food and water to be the medical treatment of a disease. Provision of food and water is normal or ordinary supportive care." Harris CE, Orr RD. The PVS debate: Even evangelical doctors may differ on this crucial issue. *Today's Christian Doctor.* 1999;30(1):8–13. Also the U.S. Conference of Catholic Bishops, "The Ethical and Religious Directives for Catholic Health Care Services, 5th ed." (2009), no. 58.
16. Former Surgeon General C. Everett Koop, along with the Association of American Physicians and Surgeons, filed papers arguing against withdrawal of the feeding tube. "The clear object of the petition here is to end the life of Ms. Cruzan, an intent which is inimical to the very nature of medicine." Brief for the Assoc. of Am. Physicians and Surgeons. Cruzan v. Director of Missouri Department of Health, 497 U.S. 261(1990)(No. 88–1503).

17. "By definition, a patient in an irreversible coma cannot eat and swallow and thus will die of that pathology in a short time unless life-prolonging devices are utilized to circumvent the pathology. Withholding artificial hydration and nutrition from a patient in an irreversible coma does not introduce a new fatal pathology; rather it allows an already existing fatal pathology to take its natural course." Father Kevin O'Rourke, The AMA statement on tube feeding: An ethical analysis. *America: The National Catholic Weekly.* Nov 1986;22:321–4.

18. Gostin L, Weir RF. Life and death choices after Cruzan: Case law and standards of professional conduct. *Milbank Q.* 1991;69(1):143–73

19. Sullivan Jr. RJ, Jr. Accepting death without artificial nutrition or hydration. *J Gen Intern Med.* 1993;8(4):220–3.

20. Printz LA. Terminal dehydration, a compassionate treatment. *Arch Intern Med.* 1992;152(4):697–700.

21. Casarett D, Kapo J, Caplan A. Appropriate use of artificial nutrition and hydration—fundamental principles and recommendations. *N Eng J Med.* 2005;353(24):2607–12.

22. Palecek EJ, Teno JM, Casarett DJ, Hanson LC, Rhodes RL, Mitchell SL. Comfort feeding only: A proposal to bring clarity to decision-making regarding difficulty with eating for persons with advanced dementia. *J Am Geriatr Soc.* 2010;58(3):580–4.

23. Reisberg B, Ferris SH, de Leon MJ, Crook T. The global deterioration scale for assessment of primary degenerative dementia. *Am J Psychiatry.* 1982;139(9):1136–9.

24. Friedrich L. End-of-life nutrition: Is tube feeding the solution? *Ann Longterm Care.* 2013;21(10).

25. Finucane T, Christmas C, Travis K. Tube feeding in patients with advanced dementia: A review of the evidence. *JAMA.* 1999;282(14):1365–70.

26. Lynn J, Harrold J, Schuster JL. *Handbook for Mortals: Guidance for People Facing Serious Illness,* 2nd Edition. New York: Oxford University Press; 2011:169–170.

**Chapter Three: Cure Sometimes, Comfort Always**

27. Connor SR, Pyenson B, Fitch K, Spence C, Iwasaki K. Comparing hospice and nonhospice patient survival among patients who died within a three-year window. *J Pain Symptom Manage.* 2007;33(3):238–246.

28. Lynn J, Harrold J, Schuster JL. *Handbook for Mortals: Guidance for People Facing Serious Illness,* 2nd Edition. New York: Oxford University Press; 2011:1–14.

29. Vick JB, Pertsch N, Hutchings M, et al. The utility of the surprise question in identifying patients most at risk of death. Presented at: 2015 Palliative Care in Oncology Symposium; October 2015; Boston, MA.

30. Wright AA, Keating NL, Ayanian JZ, et al. Family perspectives on aggressive cancer care near the end of life. *JAMA.* 2016;315(3):284–92.

31. Callahan, D. *The Troubled Dream of Life: In Search of a Peaceful Death.* Washington, DC: Georgetown University Press; 1993:201–2.

32. Aldridge MD, Canavan M, Cherlin E, Bradley EH. Has hospice use changed? 2000–2010 utilization patterns. *Med Care.* 2015;53(1):95–101.

33. Wolfe J, Klar N, Grier HE, et al. Understanding of prognosis among parents of children who died of cancer: Impact on treatment goals and integration of palliative care. *JAMA.* 2000;284(19):2469–75.

34. McCabe MA, Rushton CH, Glover J, Murray MG, Leikin S. Implications of the patient self-determination act: Guidelines for involving adolescents in medical decision making. *J Adolescent Health.* 1996;19(5):319–24.

35. American Academy of Pediatrics Committee on Bioethics. Guidelines on forgoing life-sustaining medical treatment. *Pediatrics.* 1994;93(3):532–6.

## Chapter Four: Treatments to Consider—Practical Help for Decision Making

36. Lacey D. Tube feeding, antibiotics, and hospitalization of nursing home residents with end-stage dementia: Perceptions of key medical decision-makers. *Am J Alzheimer's Dis Other Demen.* 2005:20:211.

37. Heunks LM, van der Hoeven JG. Clinical review: The ABCs of weaning failure—a structured approach. *Crit Care.* 2010;14(6):245.

38. Ankrom M, et al. Elective discontinuation of life-sustaining mechanical ventilation on a chronic ventilator unit. *J Am Geriatr Soc.* 2001;49(11): 1549–54.

39. Wong SP, Kreuter W, O'Hare AM. Treatment intensity at the end of life in older adults receiving long-term dialysis. *Arch Inter Med.* 2012;172(8): 661–3.

40. Davison SN. End-of-life care preferences and needs: Perceptions of patients with chronic kidney disease. *Clin J Am Soc Nephrol.* 2010;5(2):195–204.

41. Kurella TM, Covinsky KE, Chertow GM, Yaffe K, Landefeld CS, McCulloch CE. Functional status of elderly adults before and after initiation of dialysis. *N Engl J Med.* 2009;361(16):1539–47.

42. Span P. Learning to Say No to Dialysis. *The New York Times.* March 27, 2015.

43. United States Renal Data System. 2015 USRDS annual data report: Epidemiology of kidney disease in the United States. National Institutes of Health, National Institute of Diabetes and Digestive and Kidney Diseases, Bethesda, MD, 2015.

44. O'Connor NR, Dougherty M, Harris PS, Casarett DJ. Survival after dialysis discontinuation and hospice enrollment for ESRD. *Clin J Am Soc Nephrol.* 2013;8(12):2117–22.

45. United States Renal Data System. 2008 USRDS annual data report: Atlas of end-stage renal disease in the United States. National Institutes of Health, National Institute of Diabetes and Digestive and Kidney Diseases, Bethesda, MD, 2008.

46. Renal Physicians Association and American Society of Nephrology. *Shared Decision Making in the Appropriate Initiation of Withdrawal from Dialysis: Clinical Practice Guideline,* 2nd Ed. Rockville, MD: Renal Physicians Association; 2010.

47. Matlock DD, Stevenson LW. Life-saving devices reach the end of life with heart failure. *Prog Caridovasc Dis.* 2012;55(3):274–81.

48. Bevins MB. The ethics of pacemaker deactivation in terminally ill patients. *J Pain Symptom Manage.* 2011;41(6):1106–10.

49. National Hospice and Palliative Care Organization. *Pain at the End of Life—Common Questions.* Caring Info. http://www.caringinfo.org/files/public/brochures/EOL_Questions.pdf. Published 2013. Accessed March 1, 2016.

50. Fine RL. Ethical and practical issues with opioids in life-limiting illness. *Proc (Bayl Univ Med Cent).* 2007;20(1):5–12.

51. Azoulay D, Hammerman-Rozenberg R, Cialic R, Ein Mor E, Jacobs JM, Stessman J. Increasing opioid therapy and survival in a hospice. *J Am Geriatr Soc.* 2008;56(2):360–1.

52. Olsen ML, Swetz KM, Mueller PA. Ethical decision making with end-of-life care: Palliative sedation and withholding or withdrawing life-sustaining treatments. *Mayo Clin Proc.* 2010;85(10):949–54.

## Chapter Five: The Journey to Letting Be—The Emotional and Spiritual Issues

53. Fusgen I, Summa JD. How much sense is there in an attempt to resuscitate an aged person? *Gerontology.* 1978;24(1):37–45.

54. Tresch DD, Neahring JM, Duthie EH, Mark DH, Kartes SK, Aufderheide TP. Outcomes of cardiopulmonary resuscitation in nursing homes: Can we predict who will benefit? *Am J Med.* 1993;95(2):123–30.

55. Justice C. The "natural" death while not eating: A type of palliative care in Banaras, India. *J Palliat Care.* 1995;11(1):38–42.

56. Stoddard S. *The Hospice Movement: A Better Way of Caring for the Dying.* New York: Random House, Inc.; 1991:xii.

57. Mitchell SL. A 93-year-old man with advanced dementia and eating problems. *JAMA.* 2007;298(21):2527–36.

58. Sonnenblick M, Friedlander Y, Steinberg A. Dissociation between the wishes of terminally ill parents and decisions of their offspring. *J Am Geriatr Soc.* 1993;41:599–604.

59. Thomasma DC. Reflections on the offspring's ethical role in decisions for incompetent patients: A response to Sonnenblick, et al. (editorial), *J Am Geriatr Soc.* 1993;41:684–6.

60. Rinpoche S. *The Tibetan Book of Living and Dying.* New York: Harper; 1992:34–5.

61. Koch KA, Rodeffer HD, Wears RL. Changing patterns of terminal care management in an intensive care unit. *Crit Care Med.* 1994;22:233–43.

62. Callahan, D. *The Troubled Dream of Life: In Search of a Peaceful Death.* Washington, DC: Georgetown University Press; 1993:149–151

63. Finucane TE, et al. The incidence of attempted CPR in nursing homes. *J Am Geriatr Soc.* 1991;39:624–6.

64. Becker, E. *The Denial of Death.* New York: The Free Press, 1973.

65. Singh, KD. *The Grace in Dying: How We are Transformed Spiritually as We Die.* New York: HarperCollins, 1998.

66. Callahan D. "Death: 'The distinguished thing.'" *Hastings Center Report* 2005;35(6):S5–S8.

67. Niebuhr, R. "The Serenity Prayer" (1934), quoted in *Familiar Quotations,* 16th Edition, edited by John Bartlett, Justin Kaplan, Boston: Little, Brown and Company, 1992:684.

68. Rinpoche S. *The Tibetan Book of Living and Dying.* New York: Harper; 1992:33.

69. Psalms 103:14–16.

70. Dunn H. *Light in the Shadows: Meditations While Living with a Life-Threatening Illness,* 2nd Edition. Naples, FL: Quality of Life Publishing Co.; 2005:67.

71. Frankl VE. *Man's Search for Meaning.* New York: Washington Square Press; 1984:90.

72. Flannery O'Connor letter to Betty Hester, June 28, 1956. *The Habit of Being: Letters of Flannery O'Connor.* New York: Farrar, Straus and Giroux; 1979:163.

73. Nuland, SB. *How We Die: Reflections on Life's Final Chapter,* New York: Alfred A. Knopf; 1993:138–139.

74. Stoddard S. *The Hospice Movement: A Better Way of Caring for the Dying.* New York: Random House, Inc.; 1991:204–205.

75. Rinpoche S. *The Tibetan Book of Living and Dying.* New York: Harper; 1992:95.

76. Stoddard S. *The Hospice Movement: A Better Way of Caring for the Dying.* New York: Random House, Inc.; 1991:211, 225.

77. Hillesum E. *An Interrupted Life and Letters from Westerbork.* New York: Henry Holt & Co.; 1981:155.

78. Quoted in: Petersen D. "Where the Phantoms Brood and Mourn." *Backpacker.* 1993;21(7):40–8.

79. Siegel B. "Laughing Matters" (interview). 1990;6(4):127–39.